T0194248

Zoe Died. What Now?

Finding Hope in Times of Loss

Dennis J. DeWitt

WESTBOW
PRESS®
A DIVISION OF THOMAS NELSON
& ZONDERVAN

THE HOLY BIBLE, NEW INTERNATIONAL VERSION®, NIV® Copyright © 1973, 1978, 1984, 2011 by Biblica, Inc.® Used by permission. All rights reserved worldwide.

WestBow Press books may be ordered through booksellers or by contacting:

WestBow Press
A Division of Thomas Nelson & Zondervan
1663 Liberty Drive
Bloomington, IN 47403
www.westbowpress.com
1 (866) 928-1240

ISBN: 978-1-9736-3069-2 (sc)
ISBN: 978-1-9736-3068-5 (hc)
ISBN: 978-1-9736-3070-8 (e)

Library of Congress Control Number: 2018907002

Print information available on the last page.

WestBow Press rev. date: 06/14/2018

About the Cover

Over the years we have had little dogs. This book demonstrates that I love dogs and the pain that is experienced when the dog dies. Is there such a thing as doggy heaven? That theological issue will be explored as well as other aspects of our faith journey.

Contents

Foreword

In this book about grief and loss are a number of true stories. Some include grief over the death of a dog and others are stories of the loss of a beloved person. The thread that is woven throughout this book is that the death of a dog or close person triggers emotions and memories of previous losses.

Interviews were conducted with a number of people who were willing to share their story and pain.

A few names have been changed.

In our 46 years of marriage my wife and I have had dogs for forty-three of them. Now, we babysit Riley "our grand dog." For reasons of practicality and with my health and safety in mind, we resist a constant temptation to get another dog.

Acknowledgments

Dr. Betsy Sunde MD.PhD -for insights and perspectives on grief and loss.

Jack Hyde editing early on, setting a tone.

Harley Brown editing later, confirming style.

Carole Lake drawings of dog personalities.

Judi Smit, perspectives on other losses, i.e. Handicaps.

members of HASP writing class

all of the individuals who were gracious to share their story.

My Wife Mary for patience and understanding, with discernment when stuck.

Introduction

At a recent writer's conference held in Holland Michigan, author Barbara Brown Taylor had a suggestion for people introducing themselves in a small group. Usually a person is asked to share their vocation, church or expectation of the meeting that day. Ms. Taylor posed the following, "Tell me about one of your scars."

Some took her cue literally. A few women lowered the waist of their slacks to expose their cesarean scars. I recalled being seven years old, falling on railroad tracks resulting in a one-inch scar because the doctor used staples, rather than stitching. Many of us have physical scars but, over time, we all carry a variety of emotional scars.

Some can remember going to the vet and asking him/her to "Take their dog, Sam, to Jesus." We talk about having to "put down" our dog. Those words trigger memories like the following:

> In 1974, I drove to Ann Arbor Michigan to submit my master's thesis to complete my degree in School Social Work. When I arrived, my instructor told me her dog died that morning. While I felt sad for her, I really wanted to bring closure to my project, so I asked if she needed any other information to give me a grade. She told me the course was pass/fail, and there were no grades. My grade point average was quite high at that point and I was looking for an "A." Instead of sharing in her grief, I focused on my needs and had failed to properly acknowledge her loss. She reiterated it was only pass/fail and that I passed. That was

forty-three years ago, but now I still have vivid memory of seeing her cry. She was a single woman, probably in her late 50s, and she had the dog for fifteen years. She told me the dog was her best friend. That "A" is not so important now. Her grief is what lingers.

Grief work is hard work. I first heard this story from Dr. Frank Freed at a conference in California.

A chrysalis is formed and a butterfly emerges through a natural birth process. If you cut the end of the chrysalis making it easier for the butterfly to emerge, the butterfly dies very soon afterwards, because he needs a special coating that comes with the birth process. Additionally, the butterfly has no color. The butterfly is the symbol of new life. It is image that young children, as well as adults can understand.

There are differences in the experiences of loss between losing a pet or losing a beloved person. Even *when a pet dies, we revisit previous losses.* That does not mean that we haven't grieved those losses, but rather that it triggers the memory of those previous losses. When our last dog died, I sobbed on the vet's shoulder. He explained I was reliving previous losses.

When losing a beloved person, it triggers a series of events. We plan a memorial service or funeral, select Scripture passages, and suggest stories of the person's life. We plan a luncheon reception and choose a time for visitation either before the service or another date. This involves extended family, close friends, clergy, musicians and ushers. Some of these tasks are processed by a funeral director. There is a time set aside for this, allowing the grieving persons movement towards some form of closure.

When a dog dies, things are different. There is usually a relationship between the dog's owner and the veterinarian. Family members may support each other in grief, but there is usually no established ritual for bringing closure. As a minister, I have been invited only twice to be present at the burial of a family dog. In comparison, in my twenty years of ministry, I participated in 124 memorial services.

When meeting with the family of a person who has died, the subject of eternal life is a focus of the discussion. On the other hand, "Do dogs go to heaven?" is a valid question. I will attempt to answer it at some point. For the most part, the stories shared are about people, people experiencing the scars of loss. As you read, look for ways to bring healing and comfort in your own story.

We are on a journey of learning

After reading *The Celestine Prophecy* by James Redfield, I became aware how we have encounters of a spiritual sense. Writing this book is then that kind of journey. As I go to social gatherings and indicate that I am writing about grief and loss, I find most people have a story to tell. The search goes on.

As Christians, we are on a journey. There is a gradual unfolding of the story as we wade through Old Testament writings and then, through the New Testament, learn of Jesus's teachings and the journeys of Peter and Paul. I believe that we are on a course of exploration every time we go to worship or study the Word. The unveiling of the story becomes especially significant if what we do during the week coincides with what we do on Sunday. My grandmother spent Saturday preparing her Sunday school lesson. Regarding the Sabbath, she was peeling potatoes, setting the table, and putting out fresh napkins along with baking the unleavened bread for communion.

Can your dog know what day of the week it is? Certainly, the dog knows a change in pattern. And when there is a predictable routine, the dog gets used to certain things. All of our dogs reacted to the suitcase coming out of the closet. They knew they were going to "camp" and would be having a good time. How did we know the dog was reacting? The dog would pace back and forth and show anxiety. We thought we knew what the dog was feeling. The dog was not able to express that with words, but only with actions. As a retired minister, I think back to the saints who went before us. Those memories are a background for the material that follows, and they speak to the grief I have felt when one of our dogs died.

〇

A 51-year-old man was outside mowing the lawn. He was a policeman. A drug sniffing dog was part of his household having lived with the family for the past five years. The man suffered a widow maker heart attack. The question then becomes, does the dog remain in the household? The chief of police allowed the dog to stay. If the decision were made to move the dog to a new home, the widow would've lost her husband and the dog at the same time. Setting aside a consideration for the cost of training the dog, the decision was made based on emotion and the well-being of the family rather than finances.

When something like this happens suddenly, the kind of decisions that are made sometimes are rather impulsive. Often the following are suggestions in such a case:

- **It is best not to sell costly items immediately, give it some thought. Such items might be a home, jewelry, a car, boat or a cottage.**
- **Drinking alone can lead to over indulgence.**
- **Find a financial advisor that you can trust.**
- **Follow up on the offer of the clergy to talk through your grief. Remember that people revisit previous losses. For some, that is more involved than others.**

1

A few thoughts on remembrances of saints who have gone on before us

I awaken in the morning, look out my bedroom window, and see a clear pond with a center sprayer shooting water up to aerate the water. When I drive past the pond at church, I see scum on the top and I remember Marv would get into his hip boots, wade into the pond, and apply copper sulfate, bringing clarity to the water.

§

If you were to phone his wife, Dorothy, you would get an answer saying "Yel-lo."

§

As I visited his sister Marie in the nursing home, I would remember she had a massive stroke and could no longer talk. She would get up and go to the dresser drawer and pull out music, singing with perfect pitch, "Mine eyes have seen the glory of the coming of the Lord." I'm not sure she could sing before the stroke, but certainly she sang with clarity now.

§

Little did we know that when I performed the wedding for Owen and Phyllis Ann, with Owen singing "love Me Tender," we would soon be attending his funeral. After Owen's death, Phyllis Ann found it difficult to come back to church in the sanctuary with a traditional setting, because there were strong remembrances of Owen there. She is now attending a contemporary worship service that meets in the gym. For many, an anniversary triggers deep emotion. For some, sitting in the same space as the funeral causes deep pain.

§

An informal conversation with Bill brought out the fact that Bill's five-year-old grandson died of a blood disease. With tears, he said a day does not go by that he doesn't think about this boy.

§

Listening to Matthew speak, I did not realize that on three occasions he lost his job in one city, procured a job in another city, and had mortgages on houses in two cities. These changes brought loss that needed processing. Fortunately, he was a man of faith and trusted God through prayer to guide him. That led him to become active in the church and go to various Bible studies, and now in retirement, he volunteers as a leader for Bible Study Fellowship. This included traveling as far away as Australia, Africa, and California.

§

A retired radio announcer from Chicago shared George Carlin's words, "The day you buy a dog, you set yourself up for grief." This man said he has grieved more deeply for the loss of his dogs than for the loss some of his relatives.

§

Why do I include the stories in this book? I have many remembrances of the people I served it would be my hope that some of the stories would trigger for you some remembrances. In doing so, you may find the activity near the end of this book helpful to define losses by decade and then evaluate the significant losses and less significant losses.

2

Happiness is the day

It has been said that happiness is the day the dog dies and the children move out. These words were spoken by a man who had two sons and a dog and was looking forward to an empty nest. This might have been true for him, but for a single person who has a dog as a companion, the grief is deep and long-lasting

Dogs need attention. They need to be fed, walked, groomed, and at times, engaged in play. A cat in the household is pretty much self-sufficient, eating when he or she feels like it and using a litter box.

Dogs become a vehicle for getting to know your neighbors.

"May I pet your dog?"

"What is your dog's name?"

"How long have you had your dog?"

"What breed is he?"

"Where did you get him?"

Unlike cats, dogs need to be attended to with things like food and walking. They have a routine.

My office is in the front of a condo. I overlook the street with mailboxes out in front. At about nine thirty or ten o'clock, the mail truck comes and I go out to get the mail. For the last three years I've been doing that alone. Prior to that, our dog Zoe would come to me as if to say, "The mail's here!" That meant that she would go out and relieve her bladder—and frequently get a treat when she came in.

OVER THE YEARS WE'VE HAD FOUR DOGS: DAISY, TOBY, MUFFY, AND ZOE. EACH ONE HAD HIS OR HER OWN PERSONALITY, AND EACH HAD A STORY TO TELL. WE BEGIN THE STORY WITH DAISY, OUR SON JIM'S DOG.

3

Our first experience with a dog

In January 1972, Daisy Alice entered our home as a birthday gift for our son Jim. Jim's birthday was the previous December, and he was going to be able to choose his own puppy. As a family we went to Iowa for Christmas, so he had to wait until after we returned to make the choice. The whole family gathered in the wood-paneled station wagon to go to Coopersville, where there was a new litter of puppies. Because it was Jim's birthday gift, it would be his choice. Once he had made a choice, the breeder indicated that the particular puppy was the runt of the litter, and thus, that another choice needed to be made. We brought home a new puppy, and she was a unique breed called an American Daisy dog. This was a specific breed of shih tzu, lhasa apso, and terrier. We were told the dog did not shed and would be very affectionate. When we got home, Jim was able to spend precious time alone with Daisy, since it would be his dog but would also be shared with six brothers and sisters. Her middle name was Alice. Being a large family, we watched *The Brady Bunch* on television. Alice was their housekeeper, so we had our own Alice.

One of the hints that the breeder suggested was that any pet becomes the bottom of the pecking order. Therefore, a dog is good for a family. Entering our family, Daisy was integrated with the various activities, traveling, camping and just hanging out. Every Thursday we had a family meeting. During those meetings, we would determine the various tasks that were to be accomplished each week. One focus became Daisy. We specified "Daisy dog days": If you were assigned to a Daisy dog day, then you then had to walk the dog, feed Daisy, and work alone in the kitchen with mom. The dog got to sleep with you that night. A tag on the doorknob would say "Daisy sleeps here tonight."

If there were ever a time for a do-over, it would be with how we handled Daisy's later life. Large dogs often live to be ten to twelve years old, and small dogs can live longer. Daisy lived to be eighteen and a half years old; she was eventually crippled with arthritis, and climbing stairs was especially difficult. As a family, we discussed the fact that she was aging, and that someday she would have to be put to sleep. One day as I was eating my breakfast cereal, Daisy "dropped a load" next to my shoes—a totally uncharacteristic behavior for her. My response was to call the vet to make an appointment to have her put to sleep. I did that in isolation, telling no one. Later that afternoon I went to the veterinary office, and the vet put her to sleep. I made arrangements for her to be buried at Noah's Pet Cemetery in Grand Rapids, Michigan. From there, I went to the school where my wife was teaching and told her what I had done. Looking back, I realize that my actions were not fair to my family:

- Daisy was Jim's dog, and he was not given an opportunity to participate in the process—or to even say goodbye.
- Family members were not given an opportunity to say goodbye.
- The process I followed was rather unemotional.
- Looking back, I feel I did not properly grieve that loss.
- It would've seemed appropriate to call a family meeting to discuss what needed to happen. I took lone responsibility for the action.
- We held no ceremony, nor has the family ever gone to Noah's Garden. The vet took care of all the arrangements and we paid for the costs, detaching ourselves from the emotion of loss and grief.

Author Note: This chapter appears to be a good beginning point for this book because it reflects my upbringing in a family that did not discuss such as issues as. Death and dying. A chapter discussing this comes later. ℵ

As I was riding my bicycle home from a condo board meeting, I was greeted by two women who are neighbors. When I indicated the kind of book I was working on, they both said they were dog people. The one woman indicated that when her dog died that she and her husband had a pact that whoever died first would have the cremains of the dog. When this woman's husband died and their son was aware that there may be a difficulty in including the dog's cremains with the father's remains, they decided that there would be a nicely decorated box. The son told the funeral director that The box contained "love letters from mom."

4

A perspective on grief in our family.

I grew up in Muskegon Heights, Michigan. Our dogs were always outside in a pen. One name that I remember particularly was "Rotterdam Rock." Rocky was a purebred beagle hound that had registered papers. The purpose of this dog was purely for hunting. This dog would go to some of the extended family property in Grand Haven, at a place called uncle Ben's farm. Uncle Ben was my father's uncle and he had the property now considered a Centennial farm. In those years, hunting was a solitary recreation. My dad would put the dog in the car and go hunting either alone, or with one other person. Occasionally he would shoot a rabbit or a pheasant. On one occasion, he came home with a partridge.

Typical of our family, there was little conversation. Occasionally the dog was allowed to come inside the house, for very short visits. Since the dog was in a kennel, he only stayed outside, unless we had subzero temperatures.

I remember one of our dogs produced a number of puppies. These were all sold for some profit, because they were purebred dogs.

In his 50s, our father gave up hunting. He would go fishing, and sometimes go on a "getaway weekend with the guys." At that time, the dog pen was dismantled and the space was used to extend the garage into a laundry room and bathroom.

That building project was a major undertaking. The ground was being prepared for the new project and had to have all the metal milk crates removed. They had been planted around the perimeter of the dog pen. Beagles are diggers and many times our dog would get out until finally the new design incorporated the metal milk crates.

Death and loss were not discussed as I was growing up. I have no memory of going to a funeral home visitation. One recollection I have, is that my mother would always get a plant for a family and bring it to the funeral home visitation herself, rather than having a florist deliver it. Was that an issue of trust or was it a cost factor?

Grief for my mother meant going to the bedroom, withdrawing from the family, crying, and staying cloistered alone for a significant amount of time. It was never considered appropriate to talk to someone about your grief. In fact, whenever I would go and talk to my aunt and uncle, who lived two blocks away, I would be accused of "airing the family wash." My aunt and uncle were people I could talk to, but I knew that there was a limitation on what I could say. Somewhere my conversation would be shared with my parents.

There almost seemed to be a sense of protection from life issues in our household. The language that was used in our house was indicative of some of that protection.

We were a church going family and participated in worship on Sundays. Funerals were often held at the funeral home, rather than in the church, but a luncheon would be provided at the church after the service.

A few years ago, when my father died suddenly of a heart attack, mother had no wish to see his body. Therefore, there was no open casket for visitation. My two brothers and I spent private time with the casket open.

When my wife Janna died in 1970 I found that much of the family didn't know how to respond, at least my side didn't know what to say or do. Two weeks after her funeral, I spent all of Labor Day writing thank you notes with no phone calls, no visitors and no outside food brought in. I was alone with four children ages, seven, five, three and eight months. Some years later, when I became a minister I was more intentional to making contact, checking in to see how someone was doing.

As we celebrated Christmas in December 1977, my father put his hand on my shoulder and said "Denny, you're doing a good job." He died two months later, shoveling snow off from a flat roof. My two brothers did not hear that affirmation. My older brother felt deep loss at the funeral, because he felt that his father was not the man he had hoped for.

Giving the blessing is a very significant part of our lives where we affirm our children, grandchildren and others that we are blessed to nurture. Having given the blessing, we then do not feel so much guilt when a person dies.

Likely the most significant two days of my life were in a silent retreat at the St. Lazares Retreat House on Spring Lake, Michigan. I went there with the suggestion of a psychologist I respect. He said I had too many voices in my head and needed to unload some. During the two days, I had a prayer book, and I did some considerable forgiveness work. Thursday night I was exhausted. I could no longer keep silence. I went to my car to get my portable FM radio and heard the <u>Faure Requiem</u>.

On Friday, I spent the entire day in prayer and silence, and at about three PM went to the Spring Lake cemetery just around the corner, to have a conversation with my parents. I asked for forgiveness for the unkind things that I had done and forgave them for things that they had done to me. This became one of my most freeing experiences, as I no longer had to carry an agenda of anger and disappointment. I knew that my parents did the best that they could, given the resources they had. When I finished the conversation, I went to my car. Playing on the FM station was the music**"Rigaudon" by Andre Campra**, with very bombastic organ that brought me to tears. Those tears were therapeutic. I went from there to the elementary school "fun night" with our children, certainly a contrast with the silence I experienced.

The physical act of going to the cemetery allowed me to talk freely about some things I was doing, sharing my spiritual journey through seminary and coming to the point of saying "I'm sorry" and "it's time to move on." Being raised in a system of reward and punishment I found this encounter to be an opportunity to bring closure to several issues. These issues were unloading some guilt, sharing my faith, and sharing my gratitude for all I was experiencing with Mary, my wife. I knew my older brother was dying and I shared that with them. When you go to the cemetery there is a one way conversation. This conversation allowed me to look realistically at what was in the past. It gave me the opportunity to go forward with my life without the impact of their judgment.

A waitress in a restaurant once said "Stillwater runs deep and dirty." In our family, there probably were some secrets that were never discussed. The silence at the dinner table was deafening. I went to college to get trained so that I would not have to continue growing up in such a private family and from a city with little potential for growth.

5

What time is supper?

The dog knows. Dogs are well acquainted with the Skinner Operant Conditioning*. There are routines that we establish around our house that the dog recognizes as cues. An alarm going off in the morning says it's time to get up. Hearing the clock chime twelve means it is lunchtime. If I go to the refrigerator, later in the afternoon to get a snack, the dog immediately responds wagging its tail. When the doorbell rings dogs respond in a variety of ways. Some come rushing to the door barking. Others just sit and wag their tail.

Some years ago, we attended the play <u>Sylvia</u> at the Hope College Summer Repertoire Theater. When the doorbell would ring the woman playing Sylvia would run to the door and say "hi" hi, hi, hi, hi, hi. Greeting a new person, our dog is saying the same thing.

When the dog has established a pattern, when she is gone, we miss the dog's presence

When the mail truck comes around the corner the engine sound is very distinct, and the muffler makes a specific noise. When I'm working in my office I hear the mail truck and remember that Zoe would always come to me to take her out to get the mail. That was usually in the middle of the morning and it was a good time for her to relieve her bladder. My neighbors must think I'm terribly obsessive, because I'm the first to go out and get the mail. Each day I relive Zoe saying" hi, hi, hi, hi, hi."

Our dogs became very nervous when they saw suitcases. They knew that we would be going away and that they would be going to Camp Jay. We are fortunate that we never needed to use the word "Kennel" for our dogs, because a very caring couple integrated the dogs into their household. People we know have a kennel where their dog goes, they can see the dog on their cell phone, knowing that the dog is very content there and well cared for.

What's the difference between a dog or cat? Dogs bark, and cats meow. One of the significant differences is that the cat can be left for a day or two and doesn't need to have someone check in, because food dispensers that measure the daily quotient. There is a litter box that the cat is used to using. Dogs need to get outside with some predictability. They need to be fed a specific amount for each meal. Dogs don't always stop eating if there is an abundance of food present.

*The work of Skinner was rooted in a view that classical conditioning was far too simplistic to be a complete explanation of complex human behavior. He believed that the best way to understand behavior is to look at the causes of an action and its consequences. He called this approach operant conditioning. Operant Conditioning deals with operand's - intentional actions that have an effect on the surrounding environment. Skinner set out to identify the processes which made certain operant behaviors more or less likely to occur. **Simply stated you give the allergy pill first and then the treat.**

6

John and Molly were quite a pair.

John now lives at a retirement village where he can find community. He previously lived along the shores of Lake Michigan in a summer cottage. Now he has a year- round facility allowing him to go to the cottage during the summer.

John and I had many conversations together over lunch. He always bought lunch and appreciated the time together.

Visualize Molly in the back of John's Volvo station wagon. She arrives at church at 7:50 so that John could sing in the choir, at both the 8:30 and 11:15 services. She is not only compliant, but she is a companion. During the summer, they both enjoy the cottage on Lake Michigan. Molly likes to retrieve sticks that tend to be a little bit too large.

One day, Molly retrieved one from the water, and carried it past two or three cottages and then put it down. She looked at John as if to say "How are we going to get this back to the cottage?" John picked it up, realizing it was quite heavy. He also carried it past two or three cottages. He knew that Molly wanted the stick back at the cottage, so that after about five exchanges like this, it made it to the cottage.

Generally, Molly was not always a compliant dog when it came to playing with the ball.On her sixteenth year Molly slowed down a little bit but continued to be a faithful companion to John. Over the years John used some hand signals, to elicit certain behaviors, rarely having to raise his voice. Generally, Molly was not always a compliant dog when it came to playing with the ball. Over the years, John used some hand signals, to elicit certain behaviors, rarely having to raise his voice

One finger curled towards you —means come

Whole hand up = "stay"

This is one of the most common commands used with dogs. Whenever possible a hand signal without words is suggested. Operant conditioning is useful here where the dog receives a treat for appropriately following the command.

Hand further down – lie down

One finger pointing at the dog – listen

John brought Molly home when she was a puppy and over the years he very gently trained her. Molly was a purebred yellow lab who could have been certified with papers, but John chose not to do that. He began to figure out her personality. For example, when he saw Molly chewing on his shoe, he thought she was being destructive to the shoe, but in fact she was holding onto the shoe for attention. Once John figured that out, he was able to train Molly to get a pair shoes for him. He indicated that one starts out with a voice and a hand signal and soon all one needs to use is the hand. And of course, he says hands need to be "friendly."

Molly played hide and seek with the grandchildren. As John was raising her, he always felt that it was important for her needs to be met, giving all the freedom that he could. Only on one occasion did he touch her to reprimand her. When Molly's food was put down on the floor, she would very quickly, gobble up the contents. A visiting dog took a long time to eat her food, so Molly would go over and eat the visiting dog's food. John tapped Molly in the nose and spoke very sternly to her. Molly backed off and never went past the food again.

John believes that everything living is holy. If we assert ourselves and say we know everything, we become God. Dogs give us unconditional love, and so we can say that that's a holy relationship, that we experience with our dogs.

When Molly died, John put together some memoirs. This letter is from a friend sharing his grief.

John, thank you for sharing your dog memoirs with us. We notice it's the anniversary of Molly's passing and we know the heart ache of losing his loyal companion. We read your amazing poem that described our Sophie to a T (she looks just like her) and cried as we knew it would also eventually be our future. It is summarized so beautifully. Nothing like those labs!! We hope you are able to celebrate these memories this weekend as they are such a gift. The years of life short but quality could be higher. Thanks for sharing.

Julie and Rick, children of Jo Lalley.

A POEM BY JOHN

With bowl clenched firmly in her teeth and patient big brown eyes,
Miss Molly stares imploringly she offers no disguise.
For her insulation ability … She's hoping for a treat
a click or two of leftovers would make her day complete.

If she instead gets a gentle pat, a scratch behind the head
She loves us just as much for that, as table scraps or bread
As Molly thrives on company of family and friends
She demonstrates a simple truth
that love all things transcends.
Used with permission

The following is communication between John and Molly and Bill and Jeb. This note from June 26, 2014 is from Bill. They met walking their dogs in the neighborhood and then established a strong friendship.

Dear John,

How kind of you to write to me! I, too, am sorry that you return to Michigan without our being able to say farewell. I'm very sorry to tell you that the reason we did not cross paths is that our beloved Jeb died in early April. He succumbed rather quickly to pancreatic cancer and although we miss him terribly, at least he did not suffer long. I miss you my friend and keep you in my thoughts and prayers.

Ever yours,

Bill

PS I'm enclosing a copy of a pastoral letter I wrote in our monthly church magazine. Thank you for the beautiful poem you wrote and sent to me celebrating your loving Molly. Give her my love. Bill

Dennis J. DeWitt

The minister's letter

The Lord tells us not to despise the day of small things, for they are always connected to greater things. Our family is currently going through some pain and perplexity. Our pain is not caused by the great and deep blows of the death of a beloved brother or sister in Christ. Rather, we grieve the death of one of God's lower creatures, our dog, who has faithfully devoted himself to us for 10 years. Those of you who know this, have been wonderfully understanding and comforting to us. I trust, therefore, that you will further understand my endeavor to bring some spiritual profit to you as I share how healing has been coming to us for this little wound. If my expression seems a bit scattered, you will appreciate, I trust, that it is because I write to you still in the recovery room of the soul, and therefore, perhaps not being quite as balanced as at other times. Why should we grieve the loss of the family pet? Did we make an idol of our dog, imputing to him all sorts of attributes, that he was incapable of denying, because he was a dumb beast? Where do we find comfort for our pain? Should we be strong? Wishful thinking? try to convince ourselves that he is with the Lord in heaven? Do we snap ourselves out of our delusion, and remind ourselves that he was but a beast with no soul? Let me try to share with you something of how we find comfort and healing for our pain.

Psalm 29 is a remarkable Psalm. It ascribes glory to God in testimony to seven (the perfect number) the natural or creational manifestations of God's sovereignty. Very little is said in that Psalm about God of creation, that he made all things and upholds all things by the Word of His power. If the truth be told, most of us do not have a vital grasp of this, and hence we grow anxious over practical and mundane things, while we glibly assume that all is well with our souls.

The glory of God is manifested in all of creation: (Ps.19; Romans 1;20). But what place does the lower creation have an economy of God? The word tells us that God made it all and declared it all very good. The first career of Adam, the first man, was to have dominion over the creation – a dominion he exercised by naming all the animals, designating them according to the distinctive character of each. The first animal we read in Scripture was a servant who spoke. Does that hint, as CS Lewis has suggested in his writings, that in the new heaven and earth the animals will not be present, but will be present with powers that originally had, that were removed from them when God cursed the creation, subjecting it to vanity on account of man's sin (Romans 8:20, 21)

It was the Lord who regarded the animals as having enough significance in his creation, that He instructed Noah to preserve every species of them in the ark. Wise Solomon did not despise the lower creation but saw the divinely arranged instruction even in an ant (Proverbs 6:6). He spoke of trees, beasts, foul, creeping things, and fish (1 Kings 4;33) not because he was a sentimental pantheist, but because he was a wise believer in the Lord, who related in a bright and balanced way with the creation of his God.

God does not refuse to use animals as itinerary imagery for his people, saying that his people will mount up with wings as eagles (Isaiah 40;3) 1likened them to lambs over which he is the shepherd (Psalm 23) Jesus spoke of the lilies, dressed in splendor, bestowed on them by God, and he spoke of God knowing whenever a sparrow falls to the ground (compare Matthew 10;29 and Luke 12;6)

The lower creatures that serve the Lord and his people. Balaam's ass saved that wicked prophet's life, not because an angel spoke through her but because the Lord open the mouth of the donkey to speak words of warning to Balaam (1 Numbers 22;28). then, we find Jesus writing a willing donkey in his triumphal entry into Jerusalem (Matthew 21;20)

In prophetic literature, we are told of the Lamb and Wolf peacefully co-existing(Is.65;25) while in apocalyptic literature we find images of lion, calf, and eagle, along with man surrounding the heavenly throne of God. (Revelation 4;7) We are told of trees in the new heaven and new earth (Revelations 22;2) with twelve kinds of fruit and leaves healing the nations (how much more will the fruit accomplish?).

What are we to make of this all? We should understand that the wonders of all creation manifest the glory of God (Psalm 19). These things are the outer traces of his ways (Job 26;14) We should not worship them, but neither should we hold them in contempt. If we hold these lesser things of our God in low regard, what confidence can we have and we hold the higher things such as our brethren in Christ, we are to honor above ourselves, rightly in high regard?

We note that many of my points in this letter are questions, hints, and suggestions. Where is the true answer to these questions? The sole answer is found in the wisdom, love, and power of our God. When Job was in great pain, he was full of questions and sometimes seemed to be as a man grasping at straws. When we saw God, all his questions were answered, all his tears dried in his letter state was better than his former.

One day we shall see the face of our Redeemer (Revelation 22; 4) and now, by faith, we reckon that in the light and love of his countenance, we shall have answers to our questions and a drying of all our tears. Meantime, as we try to see darkly through the glass of Scripture, I am convinced that the glory to come will not be one devoid of lower creatures but are fuller of them than is this old world that is passing away. As I humble myself to ponder the excellent virtues of the lower creatures, as Scripture tells me to do (Philippians 4;8), I am led to think that they shall not cease richly to adorn the new earth, which shall be freed from its bondage to corruption to rejoice in the glorious liberty of the children of God (Romans 8;21). I am led to think that I should hold all things of this world, especially my fellow man, God's crown of creation, in higher, not lower regard. As I follow this lead, I find peace, comfort, and hope in the wisdom, loving mercy, and power of the Lord.

Yours in his healing hand William Harrell

The following is a note to John written by Bill on the death of Molly Dated 21 August 2014

Dear John,

I weep with you, my dear friend, over the loss of your beloved Molly. Thank you for sharing this tender news with me, and especially for sending me the card of photos that preserve visual traces of her life. She was a great dog and I have no doubt that she now faces in ceaseless rejoicing with our beloved Jeb in that glorious place, for the wolf and the lamb dwell together in peace, and where we shall join them in due course. Your letter and card arrived as we are preparing to leave for Columbia South America and we just returned. I hope you are well and singing

Your brother and friend, Bill

Molly and friends have a play date

Note from the author:

Written communication like this is a real treasure. We currently are in a society where there is not necessarily a written transcript of communication. Texting on a cell phone does not bring a written copy. One might use the term "legacy "for what has transpired between John and Bill.

His story affirms the fact that dogs are connectors to other people, and that grieving for them many times is a solitary experience. John and Bill are fortunate to have each other.

All communication from Bill are used with his permission.

7

Bubbles_a story of transitions

Our church had a Parish nurse for number of years. This is her story.

One day, as I was greeting people outside of church, a woman approached me saying she had just moved to town. She had come from California and had training as a nurse. I indicated to her that we had a new program called Parish nurse, and would she be interested in learning more about that program. She said yes and long story short, she became the Parish nurse for about 10 years. She and I worked together to co-lead a grief group for recent widows. In her role as a Parish nurse, she did much pastoral work visiting people in hospitals, nursing homes, and in their home. I asked her to write about her story and what follows are her words.

Anne Writes:

I was born, and stayed, an only child. Though God blessed me with friends of the spirit and a loving family, my journey through life has always included a pet as a "side-kick." While some people remember events in their life by placing them with a home or a car that they've owned, I have always marked significant times by the pet that was with me. There were goldfish and turtles, song birds, chickens and peacocks; from goslings to goats, horses to lizards; and of course, dogs ... always dogs.

Let me tell you about Bubbles, a bright, spirited, shih tzu who unquestionably came into my life at the best time. Bubbles lived up to her name by bouncing into a room, up on a lap and on to the next, then race through the house with such joy. She lived eighteen years and was my partner, comforter, and social chairman. She accompanied me and my husband across the country to settle in a totally new home; she experienced with me my husband's sudden death and my prolonged grief. She then re-crossed the country with me as I trusted in God enough to begin a new marriage and new household. Talk about multiple transitions. Throughout it all, she was my strength and unfailing support.

I remember a time, months after my husband had died, Bubbles was sitting on my lap as we watched TV. Suddenly we both heard a deep laugh; and were surprised it was coming from me after so long a time of sadness. I remember her expression with her head cocked looking at me with joy ... well doggy joy. We shared the best of times as well as the worst, side by side.

When her time came to leave us, at 18 years, a friend gave me the kindest gift of accompanying us to the veterinarian's office to console us. Other gifts that I have appreciated over the years, and parade of pets, were those people who talked of their own memories of my pet. I am grateful to those who have recognized my grief was real even if it was for a pet; and who have affirmed that feeling grief brings out the emotions of earlier losses of pets and people. There are those who gave me a gift of time to talk about my feelings, who offered mementos such as a card or note, a book, even a warm snuggly lap shawl. All of these are still a part of my treasures.

I can only pray that all of you be blessed with a loving, attentive, joyful pet to accompany you through life.

Authors note: it was difficult for Anne to put Bubbles down because Bubbles represented her whole life history when she was married. The first loss came after 45 minutes, where husband had a heart attack. The second loss came after a period of time when her husband had cancer. Bubbles contained all that history with her.

8

Sydney

Run, Sydney Run

Bolting out the door, Sydney (an Australian shepherd, what else?) would run every chance she got. She would get her nose in the door whenever a visitor came or any of the family had to go outside. Sydney was David's full-time companion, especially once he became homebound from chronic medical problems. She was too big to be a lap dog, but would stand or sit next to David's chair, just within arm's reach so he could pet her, seemingly endlessly, even while he was napping.

But Sydney was the alpha dog and had wanderlust. Living on thirteen acres with a pond she plunged into at every opportunity wasn't enough. When she ran, she was gone for hours, once coming back at eleven pm in several feet of snow, dragging a full deer skeleton from somewhere in the woods. She wouldn't come in until she was ready, and to try to coax her in meant she would skitter off just far enough that she couldn't get caught. David's health failed and after several hospitalizations and a short stay in a nursing home, he passed away.

After David died, Sydney was there to greet Betsy whenever she came through the door and continued to try to run, in spite of Betsy's attempts to often walk her. She let Sydney sleep in her bed, something David had never allowed (there wasn't room anyway). When the daughter was visiting with her English setter, Koda, they ran off for several hours. Koda would usually stick close when he was just around the house, coming quickly when called, but he loved to run with Sydney. It turned out they both had lost their tags and were taken by the authorities to doggie jail. They were named Donna and Dallas, given unnecessary immunizations and kibble and later bailed out by Betsy. Subsequently Sydney suffered from a constant cough all night which prompted a visit to the Vet Emergency Room in the middle of the night before Easter Sunday. Betsy was not familiar with kennel cough: if she had been, she could have avoided the all- nighter in the ER.

On a Sunday afternoon in May, Betsy put Sydney on a long lead and let Koda and her out the front, thinking Koda would stay around and Sydney couldn't run past the lead. No surprise that Koda took off and Sydney after him, breaking the collar attached to the lead. They were off and gone and Betsy climbed into the car to look for them in the nearby streets. When there was no sign of them, she returned home and found them at the end of the short block near the house. Sydney was lying down and Koda was nearby. She put them in the car and took them to get a new collar for Sydney. By the time she got back home, Sydney couldn't get out of the car and couldn't walk when Betsy put her down on the ground. Another trip to the vet ER for eight hours, diagnosis unknown, three medications and advise to keep her quiet and let her walk as little as possible. After a month of medications, two chiropractor appointments, follow up with the regular vet and then a consultation with the orthopedic vet, she got a diagnosis of bilateral torn ACL's. The choices were not good, either two separate surgeries with plates and screws, immobilization a month each and lots of pain with no guarantees, constant chronic pain with very limited mobility, or euthanasia. Sydney was almost eleven years old and miserable when she couldn't be active. Betsy struggled with the decision for a few weeks, then finally decided that Sydney wouldn't want a life of chronic pain and immobility.

As is typical with nearing the end of a dog's life, we have considerations of comfort measures, and balancing cost vs quality of life. When is a decision made for the benefit of the dog or when is it postponing the inevitable?

Having Sydney put to sleep brought back memories of the woman's husband dying in a nursing home. He had several health factors that they knew would shorten his life. He was home most of the time with supportive care, but when his condition deteriorated, he finally needed to go to the hospital for extensive treatment, and then to a nursing home for twenty-four hour care. During this time there were several situations that required decisions which David and his wife were able to make together. Betsy was anxious there would come a time she would have to make hard decisions for him on her own. Soon after he was moved to a nursing home, God intervened and David passed away peacefully before more difficult decisions were forced on him and Betsy. Having to make the decision for Sydney was very difficult. It took a few weeks and weighed on her for quite a while afterwards. It helped that, after she had made the decision on her own, she felt a sense of peace.

She buried Sydney's ashes in the same spot as David's and found comfort that Sydney is enjoying romping around with David in heaven as much as he is enjoying her being with him. Now she can run, Sydney Run to her heart's content and he could run after her, having shed his imperfect body for his boundless spirit. She moved from a house to a condo, and many of the memories of Sydney remain with the house. Being alone in the condo, this woman misses Sidney greeting her when she comes home. Being a voracious reader, she has found that reading is an escape, and in some ways, covers her pain of loss. Knowing that she will retire in a little over a year keeps her focused on being able to move closer to family in the southeast.

One of her outlets is singing in the church choir. This activity becomes an introduction in any new community to a social group as well as being part of a spiritual journey.

Dogs are keepers of our emotions and thoughts in many ways. For David's family, losing Sydney was losing a connection to David, since she was "his" dog. We should honor, experience and process their loss, not just rush through it.

Author Note: Betsy lived in Holland, Michigan for several years. She worked as a child psychiatrist. She has moved to North Carolina and finds that she is able to duplicate some of the activities she had in Western Michigan with the exception of being able to do more of the things she wanted to, because she has retired. Joining a Newcomers club, establishing a relationship with the library to take books out on Kindle have given her some personal resources and some activities to be engaged. Historically she has found being in the church choir to be a good connection. She still seeking a good relationship there.

9

How do we talk to children about death?

It was Grandma's turn to take the five-year-old to buy school clothes for starting kindergarten. As they drove down the road the grandson asked, "Grandma, what is that?"

Grandma's response, "it's a cemetery."

Again, the grandchild asked, "What's a cemetery?"

Grandmother said, "That's where they bury people when they die."

Five-year-old asked, "Don't they get sand in their mouths?"

"No," Grandma responded, "They are buried in a box."

"How do they get to see Jesus?"

Grandmother said, "The soul goes to be with Jesus."

"What's a soul?"

Good question

You can guess what the conversation was when this little boy went home and talked with his mother.

In 1970, my wife, Jan, died of breast cancer. I was left with our four young children. When I told the children their mother had died, the seven-year-old cried, the five-year-old became very quiet and pensive, and the three-year-old laughed at her brother crying. The youngest was too young to comprehend.

Knowing their mother was dying of cancer I consulted with my minister and several others to get advice on how to talk to our children about death. The recommendation I received was to speak about the finality of death, and talk about eternal life. That is quite a challenge for young children to comprehend all of those concepts.

At one point the children had goldfish and another time a gerbil. These are creatures that don't live a long time, so you have an opportunity to talk about proper disposal when the fish or gerbils die.

Earlier in this book I described our first dog, Daisy dog. I have been recently reminded by my son that we had a dog named "Fritz." He was asking what happened to Fritz?

It became a very difficult conversation, because he was about three years old when we went to the dog pound and got the mixed breed dog we called "Fritz." There was not a teaching moment with this dog, because in a very short time the dog experienced distemper. I was very afraid of the dog, because he was showing irrational behavior. Living in a suburban area, I called the Sheriff's Department. They came immediately and expressed the need to put the dog to sleep because of the distemper. I made sure the children were out of the house when this was accomplished. I did not feel it proper to talk about shooting a dog, especially since we only had the dog for very short time.

With young children, one is faced with an explanation of heaven. If heaven is described as "up," then children feel the person that has died and gone up, and could come back down. If one can imagine a stairway that goes up, then children think a person could come down the stairway.

When you're speaking of heaven to small children you begin to describe the soul. The soul can be seen as our personality, our expressions when we are happy or sad, the storehouse of memories that we have of people who have died, or are still living. Immortal souls belong only to human beings. For example, the Catholic Theologian Thomas Aquinas attributed "soul" (anima) to all organisms, but argued that only human souls are immortal.

That becomes very complex for a child to understand. Some children have trouble naming their emotions and so giving permission to cry, or laugh, or be angry are all part of the grief process for children.

Naming the anger helps to process the emotion. Boys and young men often have been given ideas like, "Boys don't cry" or "Be a man." Children observe what adults around them are doing and it's especially important as a caring adult to have the message match the model.

Hospice organizations now have the opportunity for children to work out their grief in small groups or individual work. Some of them offer play therapy. Bibliotherapy is defined as reading a book with a child that helps the child express the emotions associated with grief. Art therapy many times can help a child with expressing their emotions of anger, frustration or loss. Many times, a child will draw stick figures of the family, and leave out the person that has died.

§

The following is an article that speaks to the needs of children in telling them about death.

Dealing with the loss of a pet is never easy. When dealing with euthanasia, or sudden loss due to an emergency illness or injury, the decisions that must be made and ultimate loss of the pet bring up many conflicting and difficult emotions.

When children are involved, special considerations must be made to help them understand what is going on and how to deal with pet loss and grief. This article will address planning for euthanasia, how to recognize signs of grief in children, and ways to start healing after loss.

Preparing for euthanasia

To put it bluntly, euthanasia is "death by injection" for a terminally ill, suffering animal. Many people euphemistically refer to this as "putting an animal to sleep." The finality of death is a difficult concept, especially for children under the age of five or so. Children can be confused and even frightened by the term "putting to sleep" if they see the lifeless pet after the euthanasia is performed.

When preparing for an appointment to have a terminally ill pet euthanized, it is best to speak in honest terms, at an appropriate level of detail for the child's age. Very small children need to know that this is final - the pet isn't going to wake up or come back. To say that the pet "went away" or is "in heaven" without offering any other details can also confuse children. Older children need to know the reasons why this decision is being made, and why it is humane for the suffering animal.

To be or not to be present at the actual euthanasia is a question with which many adults grapple. This is a personal decision and one that should be discussed with your veterinarian. When children are involved, some veterinarians, such as Dr. Evelyn Wilson, DVM, ABVP, do not allow children under the age of five to be present for the actual euthanasia.

Dr. Wilson feels that the very young children have a hard-enough time understanding the concept of death and that witnessing the event does not make it easier to understand or cope. She notes that even kids up to the teenage years can have a difficult time understanding the reasons why and the emotions involved with the act of euthanasia.

It is important to realize that when the humans (adults and children) are upset, the pet is, too. While difficult, it is important that the humans try to lend support and comfort to their animal friend in this last time of need. Seeing their humans upset may also upset the pet, too.

Sudden death or finding a pet dead.

For situations where the animal is fatally injured or is found dead from unknown causes, children need to be assured that the animal is no longer in pain. The shock can be more emotional than a "prepared for" death. If veterinary care was attempted, the child should be reminded that sometimes pets don't survive, despite best attempts to save them.

Signs of grief in children - warning signs

Children may take longer to grieve and "get over" the loss than adults. A short time of depression, acting out, or gloominess can be expected and should go away.

Longer periods or abnormal activity following loss should be addressed by the parent, a counselor or minister, or a grief/loss support resource. Warning signs of severe or prolonged grief will vary significantly with the variables of child's age, relationship with the pet, emotional maturity, circumstances involved with the death, and so on, but here on some general guidelines for recognizing grief in children:

not interested in usual activities
withdrawing from friends and family
eating considerably less than usual
reverting to pre-potty training or bed wetting
afraid of being alone or going to sleep, nightmares
preoccupied with thoughts of death

Talking about the death with the child is a good first step. For more assistance and guidance, know that there are many grief and loss support resources and hotlines. Many of them are free of charge, available online and in the phone book.

Moving forward - time to heal

Remembering the deceased pet

It is important never to belittle or ignore the child's relationship with the deceased pet. To say that it was "just a goldfish, and we can get a new one tomorrow" does not address the child's grief or teach the child the importance of the human-animal bond. Children often have *imaginary* friends that warrant conversations and emotions - pets are real - they warrant true feelings and emotions too! It does not matter how small or "insignificant" the pet may seem to adults.

Closure

Having a burial, memorial, or similar ceremony helps to reinforce the importance of the pet's life and mark the death event. Children should be allowed to participate in whatever way is appropriate - helping mark the grave site, decorate the urn of ashes, or draw pictures of happy times together with the pet - whatever activity fits with the closure ceremony and allows the child to say goodbye in their own way.

Getting a new pet

This is a very personal choice. Children should not be rushed into getting another pet to help them "get over" the deceased pet. One pet does

not replace another and *getting a new pet too soon may only cause the child to resent (even mistreat) the new pet.* Only once the child can speak openly about the deceased pet and shows interest in a new pet then should the subject of a new pet be discussed.

Author note: The death of a pet is a big deal to a child as is the death of a loved one. A local psychiatrist says that most of the children on the psychiatric unit report loss of a pet within the last year. Children who are depressed or angry can still grieve, they cry about the loss of a pet for years. This psychiatrist shared the preceding article from a journal with me, author unknown.

₪

Our friends dog died and they asked their minister to be present at the burial of Poochie. This is her prayer.

Lord God, you have taught us much about life and now we need to be taught about death and comforted by you.

We have sadness, an empty hole in our life because our dog Poochie was dearly loved. We know that we can live without him, but we do not want to.

Thank you, Lord, for the years of joy that we had together.

Thank you for memories of …

And now, God our Father and Creator, we leave our days with Poochie behind,

knowing that you are the lover of all creatures in your creation and that you will care for it forever. Amen

10

Therapy dog

Mary Ann brought change to a person with the use of her therapy dog at a local hospital.

I called ahead to set an appointment with Mary Ann to talk about her experience with therapy dogs, and dogs in general. When I arrived, she was concerned that the dogs did not come to greet me. Typically, dogs will come to the door and their greeting is usually "hi, hi hi." The two-year-old had been unintentionally cloistered in the garage, and he soon came out to greet me. The 18-year-old dog sleeps most of the day, but eventually did come to greet me and laid at Mary Ann's feet, continuing to sleep.

Mary Ann grew up in a home where dogs were not appreciated. After she was married her husband came home with a small package and put it on her lap. It was a dachshund that had very short legs and large tummy. That began a journey, with many dogs to follow. One of her early dogs was Frankie, who she said was" created by a committee" yet became one of their favorites.

Going through the process of grieving a dog is very difficult. Mary Ann relates that saying goodbye to them often was especially difficult. As she was leaving her house one day a huge eagle came right in view onto her windshield, and followed her along the Lakeshore until it finally flew with its massive wings on its journey. That eagle was a clear signal that Muffin, who had died, was in a safe place.

Trained as a Psychiatric Nurse Mary Ann, eventually went through the training for her dog to be a therapy dog. One day, she brought her dog to the psych unit of a local hospital were a woman was sitting on the floor in a catatonic state. The woman began to pet the dog and moved out of her isolation into interaction. The nursing staff was quite amazed at the transformation that happened. This woman was now talking, and finally came out of her room and assisted Mary Ann in leaving the unit.

There is quite a procedure in bringing a dog to the hospital. The dog must just have a bath, and even on entering the hospital Mary Ann would wash the dog's feet and make sure that he was very clean.

One of the questions Mary Ann posed was "why were dogs chosen to be closest to people?" Cats are different, cats own you. Starting out with a fear of dogs, Mary Ann is now very engaged with dogs and her children also have dogs. One of her daughters is Involved in Agility. This is in obstacle course where dogs are in competition for prizes. The trainer or family member is involved three days in a row in this activity. As we talked about all of the experiences she has had with the dogs, the most difficult is when the decision has to be made to put the dog to sleep. To counteract that Mary Ann has volunteered in an organization called "Best Friends" a no kill shelter in Arizona. There she would take dogs for a walk, hold them and of course get attached to them. When it came time for her to return home, she found it impossible to leave a blind Dalmatian, so Dolly went home and related with her eyes. Even though the dog was unable to see, she had keen sense of presence.

Mary Ann shared with me that two of her grandchildren died very shortly after being born. She said the dog would see her crying, get up in the chair, and lick the tears from her face. Not only do we as caretakers provide comfort for our animals, but our animals many times minister to us. This is all part of them giving us unconditional love.

11

Tanner

A woman I know has a fabric design business operating out of her home. She has a routine of going for a run with the dog, the dog would fall asleep, and leave her alone for the rest of the day. Tanner was about 12 years old when he started to decline in health. The family had to decide to take him to the vet center, so he would no longer suffer the problem with his hips. Immediately there was a search to find a puppy who could be rescued and cared for in this home. What a difference. Now that lady goes for a walk in the morning with Luna the dog. When they get home, the dog still wants to play. One day the lady found the dog on top of the table sunning himself. She was very conflicted, wanting to chastise the dog for being on the table. She turned around and laughed, because she found it so funny. Production in her sewing business has diminished when the puppy became part of the household.

It takes about two years for a puppy to mature and settle down. In the interim, dog obedience school can be utilized to help the dog improve its behaviors.

It takes a lot of patience to train a dog. Not only does the dog need to have an established territory, but the dog also needs to learn to relieve its bodily functions in the right places. A well fitted cage gives the dog a sense of security and knowing there are boundaries. With our dogs, when we tapped on the top of the cage, the dog would run into the cage and then we would give the dog a treat. That kind of operant conditioning gradually led to just tapping on the cage without the treat. Otherwise the dog gets fat.

12

Roxey

Grandmother, at 86, was dying of congestive heart failure. A granddaughter said about a year ago, she hoped her grandmother and her dog would not die at the same time.

Grandmother died in January and the family was given plenty of time to say goodbye. Funeral arrangements were made in advance and plans were made for a memorial service. Several family members had input to the music, the Scripture and the theme for the service. There was a time for family visitation, to say their goodbyes, and then a period of time for friends and family to express their stories.

A memorial service was held for a large number of people and included a bulletin with a picture of grandmother's story, the order of worship and an invitation to a reception following the service. All of this provided many opportunities for the family to interact, and bring formal closure, at least to this chapter.

After a struggle, the family took Roxey to be put to sleep. This was done by the father, the mother and the daughter. The son was away at college. The family came home afterwards to the extra empty house and quiet. When it was time for the mail to come, the mailman was informed that the dog would no longer be barking at him. What were counted as regular routines were now changed.

In both of these situations, there was time to prepare. With grandmother's death, interaction was with her three daughters, their spouses and all of the grandchildren. Grandmother was part of a bridge group, they came to the visitation. The grandparents were active members in their church for many years, thus these people came to the visitation, the memorial service, or both. It was winter so some of the friends were in Florida, yet there were a number of people present.

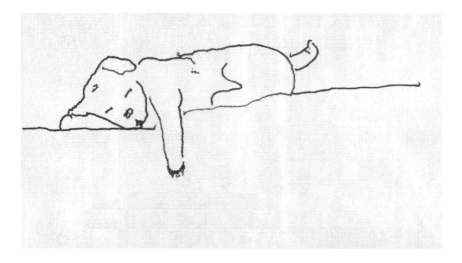

Grandfather was attentive and loving and now lost. Being a man, he was a doer. One day he got out the ladder to clean the eaves. You can predict what the next words will be. Yes, he fell off the ladder. Off to the hospital, some significant bruises and impact on the brain. He is now in an assisted living facility. The next stage is the realization that he will no longer be able to drive, another loss.

The family has a new puppy.

The journey begins anew.

13

How much do you spend on the dog?

In some cases, the money spent depends on the age of the children or the age of the dog.

Recently, four and a half pound Bella was taken to the emergency vet center because she was acting very strange. After several tests and x-rays it was determined she had a piece of metal in her stomach. Upon further examination and surgery, they discovered this was a piece of metal that came from the grill brush. It appeared she had a piece of meat scrap that had been grilled. "Table scraps" were not her usual food. As a result of this procedure, when she came home, she had lost a pound and was having difficulty recovering. Thus, another trip back to the vet center, revealed this was normal recovery behavior. A mixture of hamburger with the fat taken off, and rice became a supplement to the baby food Bella was given. With this combination, she got her energy back and has returned to her normal activity level.

How much did this cost? The response: "One could buy a really nice kitchen appliance like a top-of-the-line refrigerator, for the cost."

There is no easy answer to questions like, "How much should be spent on a dog?" It would be great if there were book where chapter forty seven would give a clear-cut answer. To my knowledge no such book exists.

There are many variables to consider:

The age of the dog. Is there a difference between a two-year-old and a 16-year-old dog?

The overall health of the dog. Will the dog survive surgery?

Is there a potential for an even worse condition?

Does the owner have sufficient resources to support further medical intervention?

Is this the family dog where young children are present?

Is further medical intervention prolonging something that realistically is not a benefit to the dog's quality of life?

It has been said dogs are like children with fur. It is difficult to separate out the financial responsibilities of owning a dog, because there is emotion involved. When one has had a dog for a number of years, emotional attachments have been made.

The financial side of having a dog is significant. From the very beginning, there are visits to the vet for evaluation and shots. Along the way there can be grooming, shots for such things as distemper and rabies. If the dog is to be taken outside the country, certification of these injections is required and a conscientious owner certainly wants to protect his/her dog from any contact diseases that may be encountered outside its normal environment. Dental care is needed for some dogs to cure bad breath; their teeth need to be brushed. Sometimes teeth need to be extracted, again a cost factor. Living in the woods for some produces the need for more flea and tick treatment.

As a dog ages, some of these costs increase incrementally. Diagnostic tests can be performed on dogs when there's a question about their health. If one has a female puppy, surgery is suggested so it cannot produce puppies. Male dogs also may have surgery to reduce their activity level. These are all options that need to be discussed with the vet.

Many dogs sleep all day as they do not know of their impending doom. Humans tend to work, and run, work out, and relate all because they know what the future might bring.

Money spent on a dog years ago was considerably less than it is today. Years ago, a dog was considered property, therefore minimum maintenance was provided. Now dogs are considered more a part of the family. Again, when the schedule changes for the family, the dog responds by withdrawing, refusing to eat or in some cases becomes even more attached to the people around.

My wife sitting in her chair quilting has an appendage, the dog is always by her side. When the dog sits next to us, she is looking for intimacy.

Dewey is part of our extended family. He needs to kiss the person entering the house when they have been gone for a period of time. The people owning Dewey sing to him when it's time to go to bed. "I love you, a bushel and a peck, a bushel and a pack and a hug around the neck."

14

What to do about grand puppies?

As a general rule, we have established that we do not invite grand puppies into our home. The following are some of the reasons: first of all, over the years we've had a dog, and many of the grand puppies are big dogs. This would overpower our small dogs. Secondly, we know the bathroom patterns of our dogs. We know that anytime our dogs can have accidents. This is exaggerated many times by the entrance of a different dog. Dog stains on carpeting are very difficult to remove. Also, the smell lingers for a long time. Any of our children are welcome to bring their dog along for a short visit. Somebody coming to the home for a birthday visit certainly feels welcome with their dog, but many times they are on edge with her dog because they don't want to offend us by messing up the carpeting or a piece of furniture.

With all that said sometimes we do break the rule. One of our sons has a medium-sized dog and likes to go camping with his family. Many of the parks do not allow pets, and so we have volunteered to take Riley for a short stay such as a long weekend. This dog is very compliant. He misses the activity of the children and so when he is at our condo, he frequently goes into his cage where he feels very secure.

When Riley arrives, he goes straight for my wife's chair where he knows he can sit beside her while she quilts or knits. This is comfortable for my wife because that is the position our other dogs kept. For the first day or so, Riley does not eat much. Might he be grieving? Certainly, there's a difference between four children under eight being active in the house, many times paying attention to Riley. Two seventy seven year-olds, have a much slower pace so it is fortunate that this dog is quite compliant, and is comfortable in his cage. We find it interesting that dogs feel more secure with some boundaries around them than just wandering around the house. Over the years we trained several of our dogs with the cage. We would use the word "cage" and tap on the top of the cage at the same time. The dog then got a treat for compliance. This is a basic example of operant conditioning. Soon just tapping on the cage brings the dog into the cage. Eventually all you have to do is tap on the cage and the dog comes running. He of course is expecting a treat, but that is withdrawn after a short time because food is a reinforcer can have a negative effect on the health of the dog.

At some time or another every one of our children has had a dog. This is probably a result of having grown up with dogs in the house. Public sentiment currently encourages people to do a "rescue dog." Some of our children have gone that route. This brings considerable neediness on the part of the dog and some very secure structure to manage this dog. When going to a known breeder, having the opportunity to choose the animal you would like, the breeder will often make suggestions or maneuver you in a certain direction. Our last dog may well have come from a breeder who had over bred this particular kind of dog. Zoe had a bulging disc in her back that the vet said may have very well come from a breading issue.

₪

A man was in downtown Chicago with his dog, and a policeman stopped him because he didn't have a leash on the dog. The owner of the dog said quote "but the dog did have a leash." Faithful to the cause the policeman started to write out a ticket. The dog's owner said to the policeman "try to get the dog to do something and see if he 'responds'." The policeman urged the dog to come, and the dog did not budge. The owner of the dog then put the dog through paces showing how the dog responded obediently to the invisible leash. The policeman tore up the ticket.

15

Talking horses and dogs, the Influence of tv and movies on our perception of animals

Some of us grew up with the talking horse Mr. Ed on television. A horse is a horse, of course of course, and no one can talk to a horse of course, that is of course, unless the horse, is the famous Mister Ed! Go right to the source and ask the horse. He'll give you the answer that you'll endorse. He's always on a steady course.

A horse is a horse of course. Many of us learned this expression years ago as we watched black and white television show called Mr. Ed. The horse had a deep voice and gave us the dialogue about what was happening around him in the barn.

Mr. Ed was suitable for all audiences. In social settings, people will imitate the voice of Mr. Ed. This TV show was on during a family hour. Parents felt comfortable watching it with their children. About the same time in television history, we also followed the family with Lassie.

A Dog's Purpose

Now we have a movie with a talking dog. "A Dog's Purpose" showing on home television sets. This movie has some relatively scary themes for young children. The whole concept of reincarnation is shown in the movie and is left up to the parents to process with their children. This dog goes through reincarnation five times with different story lines.

The movie begins in an unspecified year during the 1950s. It is then that the narrator canine begins and ends a very brief life as a feral puppy named Toby, who wonders what his purpose is.

His strong spirit is reborn and reincarnated as a newborn Retriever puppy in 1961,

Bailey reincarnates into another dog life, a female German Shepherd Police dog named Ellie, sometime in the late 1970s/early 1980s, while possessing full memories and experiences of his past lives.

Reborn again in the mid-1980s as a Pembroke Welsh Corgi, he forms a bond with an Atlanta college student named Maya who names him Tino. Maya is lonely, which Tino, having bonded closely with the girl, realizes, and makes his purpose to find her some happiness

At the conclusion of the movie, "Bailey", the dog tells the audience that life is about having fun, saving others, not getting caught up in the past and regrets, finding someone to be with and to "be here now."

These two sections are result of a Google research on the Internet. Specific chapters have been shared and edited for this book. They are included, because we often question whether animals have language. We know that dogs have receptive language of 150 words and no expressive language. Sadly, we find today that the material Roadrunner. (Roadrunner gets killed and lives again) Is that a fantasy we've grown up with?

The following two chapters utilize talking dogs. Toby was known for writing the Christmas letter, but for this purpose Toby is ministering to Elaine as Elaine's mother is dying. Dogs know about changes in the adult world and often respond with sensitivity. The chapter after Toby is "The Little White Dog"

16

Toby

They told me I was going to camp. I thought that would be better than spending time in jail, so I agreed to go. The big people here said they needed a rest, and I had a chance to try something new. Every night, at the big people's house, they would tap on the jail cell and I would be compliant go right in. Now they were packing me up, with the jail, to go to a new place.

Elaine set the rules for me when I arrived at camp. She said I could not be on the sofa, I had to sleep near the bathroom, and we would be getting plenty of exercise. I was told there were no little people at this place, so at least I would get some rest.

This place is really quiet, except when Jay gets out his trumpet to play revelry. That hurts my ears, so sometimes I let them know that the sound bothers me. Maybe it's just the fact that it interrupts my sleep!

I also found out that these people are a lot like others I know who take care of me, except that Jay and Elaine took me for rides in their car more often than others.

When I arrived, I could tell Elaine was bothered about something. She would sit at the table and work on something, but usually she would have a blank stare. I tried to get close to her, but with the rules she had, I wasn't sure how close I should get. Elaine seemed sad. I heard her say that her mother was very sick, so I tried to stay close by. She would take me to the nursing home, but I usually had to stay in the car. When she came out, she would talk to Jay about how sad she was, that her mother didn't seem to be getting better. Now I think I'm beginning to break down some walls with her. Sometimes just being close says I care, and I tried to comfort her the best I could. She talks to me, and I try to listen.

It is warmer here than at my other nights in jail. Jay spends time cutting wood and building fires in a wood stove. If they let me, I occasionally sleep near the fire to keep warm at night. I notice now that there is a blanket on the sofa, so I decide to sleep there also. As a guest, I have to be on good behavior. I wonder what I can do to repay their kindness and attention? It certainly is better than spending time in jail. I think my behavior is beginning to improve and they are letting me out for walks, without restraints. It must be that I am behaving, and they trust me more.

The food is about the same as when I'm at the other house, in jail. I have little variety. Sometimes I get a little variety with table scraps, but I think Jay might get in trouble with the jail warden, so I am polite and have just a little. I probably won't try too much new food, or I will be spoiled and have trouble returning to the same boring food at the jail place."

Someone once said that life events are not accidents. It is no accident that I am at camp this week. I was here just a few days, but during that time, Elaine's mother was very sick and died. I think I have ministered to her with unconditional love.

The nonverbal communication here tells me it's best to listen. What is most important now is my presence. Being close and getting good eye contact seems to help. Just being here has helped Elaine talk out her feelings. I've seen her relax the rules a bit, as she has been involved with her grief. I guess she just needed me to be around to help her.

As you can probably now imagine, this was written by Toby a purebred Shift Tzu a dog. We brought Toby to Jay and Elaine's home for the first time when we were on a spring vacation to Florida. They had never had a dog in their home, but because they were good friends, they agreed to take him. We were so apprehensive, that we almost called home during the week to see how he/they were adjusting. When we returned home, they suggested that we go on vacation again, because they had so much fun. (Later that year was the time when the above writing was accomplished.)

About two years later, Toby ate a corncob that didn't fully digest. He became sick on his seventh birthday, we took him to the vet that morning and by five o'clock that day he was very weak. We received a call at nine from the vet saying that he was going to do surgery for an intestinal obstruction. A few minutes later we got another call saying Toby died on the table before being given the anesthesia. We went to the vet and cried on the shoulder of Dr. Schmidt. He agreed to bury Toby in a special location. We then had to go to Jay and Elaine's to have a good cry with them, because they had become very attached to our dog. Elaine felt very responsible for his death, because they had many corncobs out for their squirrels. We also had corncobs in our neighborhood. No one can prove that he ate them at our house or theirs.

What did we learn?

When one suffers a loss, the loss represents an accumulation of many losses. I grieve for the loss of my parents, the recent death of my older brother, the death of a favorite aunt, and other un-grieved losses. When Toby died, Elaine also revisited the death of her mother, because Toby was attached to the memory of that grief process. Our first dog lived eighteen and a half years and had to be put to sleep. The expectation was that Toby would live a long life, and we were very attached to him.

It is important to properly grieve the loss of one dog before committing to another. We met with Jay and Elaine after a few weeks to decide whether or not to get another dog. We decided to proceed, thus Mary researched throughout the state to find the best breed, choosing a mixture of Shih Tzu and Lhasa Apso called "Shilazo." Elaine went along to make the choice with us. We agreed to the full-time care, purchase, shots, etc. and she and Jay would do respite care so we would never have to use the "Kennel" word.

The new dog was named "Muffy." Frequently we called him Toby, a sign we may not have properly grieved the loss of the previous dog.

We were told that when one adopts a dog, one has to expect that he/she will live longer than the old dog. One has to be prepared from the beginning to lose the dog. That caused me to detach at first from a new dog, because I didn't want to get close and then face losing him. Now after three years I made the attachment, and he has won our heart.

When the family dog "writes the Christmas letter," as strange as that sounds, he can say some things from a different perspective, and with a special humor. Ann Landers always receives letters about people who have the dog write the Christmas letter, but we have had some fun with the process.

People who like dogs, enjoy seeing the dog at their home and interact with him. Those who dislike dogs, or previously had unhappy experiences with one, preferred to stay away from them. A dog owner creates a special sensitivity to the needs of others, as they relate or dislike relating, to small pets

17

The little white dog

"I really can't figure this out. Every day I go for a walk around the large block, and people wave and are friendly. The man I walk with doesn't say much. He just diligently takes me for a walk and waves to people as they either walk by or drive by us. Sometimes one of the neighbors will stop to pet me. I know I'm cute and I wiggle my tail when someone pays attention to me. In the winter, the man puts on a warm coat, and we go for the same walk. There are no neighbors outside because of the cold weather, so it's even lonelier when the snow is flying. The man doesn't say much. He just diligently walks at a slow pace so I can do what I have to do. There's a woman in this house who stays pretty much in the house. She never takes me for a walk. I guess it's a man's job. Sometimes the man sits in a chair in the driveway watching the cars go by. Sometimes he lets me run free without a leash, always cautious that I don't run into the road.

The neighbors comment that I always look so clean. That's because they take good care of me. They say that walking the dog helps to get to know your neighbors. All the neighbor's houses look the same. There don't seem to be many children in this area, just older people.

I really like it when the dog who looks like a teddy bear is out for a walk. She's really cute and the lady that goes with her is real friendly. I wish the man who walks me would smile more often. I'm happy and content, pleased to walk the neighborhood, but he doesn't say much and just follows the same routine four or five times during the day.

I've figured out I live in a condo association where most of the people are older. People can move in with a dog, but when the dog dies, it cannot be replaced. I've made friends here, but in the last 10 years, the dog population has gone down. I used to be friends with Zoe. She died three years ago. I really miss her because she would hang out with me.

I guess I should let you know my name is "Chip." I'm not very old so I expect to be around here for a while. I kind of look like a bichon, but some might call me a miniature poodle. I like best to be called, "the little white dog" because people like me just as I am."

Author comments:

Some people have a bird or a cat for a pet. We usually don't see people walking a cat or bird. When people walk the dog, they have remembrances of locations and people. When the dog dies, many of those connections are lost.

In a recent picnic I spoke with Chip's owner. Both he and his wife said the Chip was three years old and they could expect their dog to live longer than they will. After they're gone they have a plan for the dog to be with a family member.

Addendum: The last few days we have not seen Chip. Being December, as a community we went caroling. One of the neighbors suggested visiting Chip's condo, as the man had fallen on the ice and broke eight ribs. All of the neighbors recognized the walking pattern.

18

Muffy

After a reasonable time had passed, Jay and Elaine went along to pick out an adorable puppy, shih tzu, lhasa apso mix "Muffy." We chose the name "Muffy" but they called him "Yoda." Here is his story:

"'Who is going to write the Christmas letter this year?' This is the most frequently asked question of me. Certainly, they don't expect me to do it. I don't have a history, nor would anyone listen to someone as the inexperienced as me. I don't even have an identity, since I'm often called by the wrong name."

Mary was told to spend enough time grieving the major loss of Toby, yet she said she wanted to proceed with a new experience. I still see her sad at times. Recently granddaughter Sarah called to recall an experience where Toby was featured in a video. I'll have to see the video with recollections of times past.

Muffy reflects on his predecessor Toby

Grief work is hard work. These people know intellectually about grief, because of past experiences. This loss seems to have hit so much harder. Likely, it was because Toby was so young and the loss was so sudden. He appeared healthy on Sunday, May 16, as they took him on a boat ride on his birthday. On Monday, he began to show signs of sickness. Early Tuesday morning he was taken to the hospital for emergency evaluation. The doctor ran several tests, including a barium x-ray. At noon, he was still fairly alert, and responded to his surroundings. At 6:00 p.m. he appeared lethargic and nonresponsive. A call from home to the doctor at 9 p.m. indicated that he would need emergency surgery for a bowel obstruction. Within three minutes a call came that he died before he could even be anesthetized. The infection was so severe that his body could no longer fight. They went to the hospital to see Toby, say their final goodbyes and proceed to make calls to the family.

Next, they went to Camp Jay, to help Elaine and Jay with their grief. Toby would no longer hear those trumpet credenzas. He had just been at Camp, a place he loved to go for retreat. Now all four of those adults leaned on each other for support asking what more they could have done. What if? What if they had been more careful with his food? The greatest gift of joy he gave to them was a special bond of unconditional love that will never be forgotten. Elaine had a close bond with him because he was with her during last week of her mother's illness two years ago. He had a special sense of knowing when someone was in pain, and he would reach out in a sensitive, quiet and caring way.

Theological questions arise when the young die so suddenly. With a lingering illness, there is some time for preparation, yet when the loss is so sudden, all the questions come. When grief is shared in a large family, grief is revisited so many more times.

Later, when visiting family in Pennsylvania one of the granddaughters said, "Grandpa, when you see Toby over Michigan when you're in the airplane, show him to Grandma." As a four-year-old she doesn't understand what "heaven" is. How do you explain to a small child when you don't have all the answers yourself?

Yes, we are given the events like this to test our faith and learn what we really believe. Surrounded by family and close friends, we're at work through our grief, and on with new life. I guess that's where I fit in. I guess I will have to be patient, accept the fact that it will take time to real memories, and I will in never be the same as Toby was in their lives. I'll do my best to give love and affection and to try to go to the bathroom outside when they take me for a walk.

Author speaks

Muffy died of congestive heart failure after being sick only four days. We took him to the animal clinic where they ran tests and showed that the body was shutting down. He died very much at peace. Our grandson Garrett sent us the following note when he was eight years old.

I'm sorry that Muffy died I hope this letter makes you feel better. I feel very sad that Muffy died. We went to see his grave.

Again, we are faced with the decision, "Do we buy another dog?"?"

Again, we consulted with Jay and Elaine since they provided respite for previous dogs. After three months, we began a quest to look for a "rescue dog." Realizing that one doesn't know what one is getting, we again chose a puppy and called her, "Zoe."

This name beginning with "Z" confirms she is the end of the line of dogs.

Zoe was our last dog, she incessantly played with a ball. Affectionate or playful would be the best word to describe her. She was a very gentle dog and spent most of her time sitting in the chair with Mary. Throughout the years we had her, she never was impatient with the grandchildren or visitors. One day she nipped at a granddaughter's face and we knew that was not normal. We discovered she was in deep pain with a bulging disc. She would walk around the room uncomfortable not knowing a place where she could sit down and not feel pain. We took her to the vet and Dr. Jill tried various shots and chiropractic adjustments. She felt that the only potential was for surgery and even that was not guaranteed to be successful, thus with Zoe sitting on my lap they gave her a shot to relax her and then finally a shot to stop her heart. This was very peaceful. We then proceeded to call Jay and Elaine. Jay took her in his arms brought her to his car and buried her in the same area where other dogs were.

19

The joys and sorrows of providing a vacation for dogs, and people they know.

Several years ago, we brought our dog Toby, to our friends who took care of him for a week while we were in Florida. We called it going to camp. As a result of that experience, others sought out the same resource for caring for the dog while they were away. As I interviewed this couple several stories emerged.

One of the dogs Jay and Elaine cared for was "Dutch Puppy." When it came time for the owners of this dog to go on vacation, they received a very vague response saying that someone else was going to take care of the dog. Elaine, in expressing this had considerable tears, for she never had a chance to say goodbye or in any way, be involved. Ultimately, they discovered that "Dutch Puppy" had been put to sleep. The tears come because she hurt deeply, primarily because she doesn't have a clear resolution to what happened.

Another dog they cared for was Sugar. Relaying the story of Sugar, again brought tears because she was very close to this dog. The dog had been sick for about a year or year and a half, and the father came to his two children indicating that they were going to have to put Sugar to sleep. The son and the daughter reacted differently. The little girl indicated that she handled it differently than her brother. She didn't cry all the time, but her brother cried all day long. Then they had to go to school. When the boy went to school, he said the death of the dog was more private matter, and didn't say anything to anyone, because he says one time another student had put their dog down and the teacher made a big thing of it. He said that he didn't like what she did and said he didn't want this to happen about his dog, so he didn't say anything to her. The little girl said that they now have a new dog, but she said she still is in love with Sugar saying this with tears in her eyes, because she's become very attached to the dog.

Jay, in this setting of camp, grew up on the farm and was used to his father or uncle having to put down an animal, be it a dog or calf. His father used to go out in the woods with his gun, where his uncle would put the animal in a bag and attach it to the exhaust of a car. When it came time to work with a dog that needs to be put down Jay was able to detach himself from the process. He is only acting on behalf of the owners of the dog.

On the farm, there were many animals, yet there was no intimacy with the dogs because they all were outside rather than in the home. Now, having dogs at camp, these animals at times shared the bed or slept close by.

One of the difficulties Jay and Elaine experience is when dogs are incontinent. In one case, a golden retriever needed to be carried down the stairs to relieve himself. He dribbled all over the man's shirt all the way down the stairs. The dog had been on Prednisone. This was removed from the diet. and still did not improve the situation. As a couple, they have worked closely with veterinarians who compassionately cared for these dogs while the owners were away.

When asked why they took dogs that were very sick or dying. Their response was," there's no such thing as nursing homes for "dogs." They feel very attached to the dogs having a relationship with them for several years. They treat the dog as if it were their own. This includes a willingness to sleep on the sofa to be near a dying dog or having a dog upchuck on some recently cleaned carpet.

Because of the intimate relationship they had with dogs, they find it very difficult to be in the room when the dog is euthanized. There is a graveyard on their property for a number of the dogs who died in their care, including two of our dogs, as they became very close to them.

This couple is essentially co-parenting dogs as the family goes on vacation. If the dog is near the end of life, they are in the position of having to make a decision to put the dog out to sleep. In the process, they need to be in touch with family members so that they are making a decision together, with this couple doing the actual physical act of bringing the dog to the vet. This is an emotional impact on them because they have had a number of these dogs for quite a few years. They have housed over fifty dogs in the years that they've been doing this It might be called a ministry.

I have used the word "ministry", because this is not a business but a relationship with dogs and their owners. Jay and Elaine do not expect to be paid for what they do. If the family wants to do something for them, they appreciate it. If the family cannot afford to have the dog taken care of Jay and Elaine still go ahead and do it. They love dogs and they get very attached them., but they have no permanent dog in their home. As a team, one of them will be comfortable giving shots for a diabetic dog and the other one does not feel as comfortable. If the dog has a habit of eating only once a day, when they come to Camp, Jay and Elaine divided the food into two parts so that all the animals get fed twice a day. All dogs go for long walks because Jay and Elaine enjoy exercising the dogs walking in the field. This couple experiences of full spectrum of emotion from engaging with a couple in getting a new puppy, to being present as a dog dies.

20

It is finished

Laverne Wise, John's mother was in the Bible study group. When I indicated that I was writing a book about dogs, she asked if she could submit a letter written by her son. What follows is a very sensitive letter outlining the process of his dog dying and letting people know what happened.

I figure it is only fair to send a communication to all of you who have, as of late, been wondering about the health and condition of my old friend and companion, BJ.

For the last several years, I know some of you have been afraid to ask, because of her physical difficulties and continual decline. Considering everything, I suppose it is rather remarkable she has lived as long as she did. She wasn't a pampered lapdog, by any stretch of the imagination. She trained hard for our use, slept outside summer through winter, ate dry dog food with mere bachelor food scraps on top: (to survive my cooking alone take some resilience) and hunted only as a true "zealot" bird dog can. In her prime she would hunt hard from dawn to dusk, for the prized stuff grouse, Boniswa umbrellas, down through the monkey tag elder swales of the Pine River bottom and up top in spider – web thick Aspen clear cuts of the Manistee National Forest. It seemed that she ran nonstop from the time she left the truck to the days end, save a few cool swims in the river. She quartered meticulously, busting through brush as only a springer spaniel can do, avoiding nothing but bare, non-vegetated soil. And in spite of all my failings as a dog trainer, her raw untainted instinct for finding birds provided ceaseless miracles. I can't tell you how many times that in my infinite grouse hunting wisdom, I proclaimed that "she must be on an evasive rabbit again", only to have a bird flush, as I turned to go the other direction. It was only after years of eating "humble pie" that I came to ritually confess "if her nose says that there's a bird here, there is!" Not only was her stamina great and instinct spectacular, but her toughness and sheer threshold for pain put this old rugged hunter to shame. I still remember once at quitting time I decide to check out the foot she'd been limping on, off and on throughout the day. To my surprise there was a two-inch-long thorn, pushed all the way into the flesh of her paw, which she had been hunting all day. Ouch! I can only imagine the pain from such a wound, but it obviously didn't compare to her driving intensity for the task at hand. We would end the day, her coat soaked in smelling of mire and sweat, snout bleeding from briar and thorn, snout bleeding, and docked tail still wagging from the ecstasy of it all. Because of her arthritis, poor eyesight and hearing, her field time has been greatly limited the last two years. For me, the memories are replayed every time I re-entered Michigan autumn woodlands with my Browning Auto-5 in one hand and hopes for it to flush in my mind's other. For BJ, the same memories are enough to induce the shuffling feet, wagging tail and cadence of delicate 'yips' in a sleeping dog's dreams; enough to convince me that she is still in ecstasy. In the last two months BJ's condition has decline rapidly, both psychologically and mentally. I made the difficult decision to have her euthanized. She would've been 16 years old this month, approximate112 "dog years" which I believe was really quite an achievement on her part. I will certainly miss her a lot and hope that you can also can share in these fond memories to her tribute.

Your friend John C Weiss's December 1 1995

21

The dog runs away

Tom and Becky have had six dogs and one cat in their married life. As soon as one dog dies, within a few days they adopt a new dog. They recognize that they find all kinds of dogs that need a home, and that many of them are not young dogs. Becky, with tears in her eyes, relates that of all the dogs that have had, the most grief came from Buddy who ran away. Neither Tom nor Becky can remember that they didn't have the gate closed.

When the owner takes the dog to the vet to be put to sleep they have closure. When the dog runs away, there is no closure, in fact it leaves many questions. Did the dog get hit by a car? Did someone take the dog home with them? Did the dog run off somewhere to die? These questions all arise with some guilt base for possibly not closing the gate. Did they do all they could to provide a safe place for Buddy?

Sharing the story, Becky indicated that many parents experience a significant loss as their children leave home without knowing where they are living. She related that many years ago she used some language from Transactional Analysis. Using the concept of "brown stamps" one can describe adolescent behavior many times is collecting negative behaviors. I have often used the term brown stamps, especially when a person commits suicide. That appears to be the ultimate brown stamp collecting. When a person commits suicide, many questions arise such as: what could I have done to prevent this? Or what sign should have been looking for to predict this? Why?

We know that anger suppressed, leads to depression. An accumulation of negative interactions can lead to potential suicide. Several years ago, a good friend took his life. I still have questions about what could I have done as a friend? On Friday, I called and invited him to join a small group of men our age. Saturday, late afternoon, he started the car up with the garage door closed.

Collecting positive feelings can be called "gold stamp collecting." The ultimate here for a young lady, might be being crowned "Miss America" or valedictorian of your class.

22

I don't want to go through that again

I'm not going to go through grieving another dog. Those words were spoken by Esther when her dog "Coconut" died. A few weeks later through the help of neighbor she adopted a bilingual, already trained and housebroken, rescue dog, "Cola" has become very good friend.

Esther lives about five miles from where she grew up. On the farm, they had many animals, including cats and dogs. When Esther was thirteen she contracted polio, impacting her from the neck down.

Was that a result of going to a church camp that summer? Might it have come from the Allegan County fair? There seem to have been many cases of polio reported that year.

She spent six months at Mary Free Bed Hospital in Grand Rapids, Michigan

As an adult, she worked as a medical records clerk at the Douglas Hospital nearby her home. There she met Carl, who currently was working in California. She and their dog, Jock went to California for a year until Carl could find a job in Western Michigan. He began work at Whirlpool where he continued for thirty five years. Esther was able to celebrate walking down the aisle at her wedding with the use of crutches. From that time on, she has mostly been in a wheelchair

Jack lived 19 years and traveled with Esther and Carl to California and then back to Michigan.

Next came JJ a miniature toy black poodle. He was a result of over breeding so that there was a problem with diabetes. He was allergic to grass and had many other health issues. She wasn't going to get another dog.

She was introduced to "Coconut" a white Pomeranian that she and Carl encountered as they camped in the summertime, at a nearby park. Friends have told Esther that "Coconut's" bark changed after Carl died. What did she say? "I wasn't going to get another dog."

A close friend wrote this poem about Coconut.

Dennis J. DeWitt

Oh Coconut, O Coconut
You're just a ball of fluff
But you would like to have us think
You are so very tough.

But we can see deep down inside
You're just a little softy
Even though you walk about
With airs so high and lofty.

We know you really are quite smart
On that we all agree
You are such fun, so full of vim,
You show your pedigree.

You have a sweet loving heart
It's big though you are small
You like to be in someone's lap
It makes you think you're tall.

Oh yes, you are a charming prince
As cute as you can be
And as you prance and strut about
No one could disagree.

That little, fluffy Coconut
is special beyond measure
He is the one we love so much,
A precious, loving treasure!

Written by Roy Metzgar 2009 *Used with permission of the author*

A neighbor helped Esther find "Kola" the dog who now lives with her. This was a rescue dog. The breed is quoted as being a long-haired Chihuahua. She looked at a shit tzu as a rescue dog, but the dog was already blind and the neighbor suggested that she go with the Chihuahua.

As I spent time with Esther, we looked at the chart at the end of this book, to determine where her significant losses had occurred. Very early, she indicated that her grandfather died. She was very close to him because he lived right across the street. Her father grew up in the same house as his father.

father grew up in that same house as his parents and had a house built across the street.

Esther spends most of her time alone utilizing the help of neighbors and a nephew. She is an accomplished knitter and she also does crochet. When possible, she goes to Bible study, attends worship on Sunday, and is part of the prayer shawl group.

Esther grew up with just one sister Margaret. She indicated that Margaret suffered from Alzheimer's disease and even when she had very limited speech she could relate to Coconut and say her name. Esther and Carl and Margaret and Jim would spend many evenings together going out for dinner. Jim is currently in hospice care, not expected to live very long.

Part of the aging process is at all your family and friends die. This Esther noted as she worships that and so many people she knew through the years are now gone. She was a charter member of Community Church of Douglas and she says that very few of the charter members are still alive.

23

The dog saved Fred's life

For many years Fred was a truck driver. He would travel from Michigan to California being on the road for several days at a time. Occasionally he had a small dog traveling with him as a companion. After several years Fred found that he was not living a meaningful life. His first marriage ended in divorce. His second wife gave him the ultimatum of either give up the truck driving or leave. He chose the truck driving, because he had a large mortgage on his truck, his home and his car. The marriage to his third wife lasted a very short time, because again the pattern was for him to be away from home for several stretches of time. In this case, his wife became unfaithful to him when he was gone.

As a result of all of the driving, Fred had some bad habits that he says really paid a significant toll on his health. Smoking and drinking created stress on his heart. seventeen years ago, he made a decision to go into rehab and stop drinking. This was after he lost his CDL license, dramatically reducing his income. In those seventeen years he has had eight heart attacks. Anxiety over money and depression associated with his lifestyle, caused Fred to make a decision to take his life using a gun. When Fred's dog saw what he was doing he began to bark. This was a pattern that Fred had not experienced before and he felt that the dog saved his life. His girlfriend came over and immediately escorted him to the hospital where he spent time in the psychiatric unit. It was discovered that much of his problem was related to medications. These were adjusted and he was released from the hospital. Counseling was suggested.

I first met Fred about two months ago and he seemed very eager to make a dramatic change in his life. Most significant was his commitment to going to church and turning his life over to Christ. Last week he mentioned that he was going to some classes to learn about baptism. Now in his 60s he says he was never baptized as a child nor did he feel a calling to do that when he was in his teenage years. Adult baptism signifies a relationship with Christ Jesus. Fred is on a spiritual journey that is very exciting at this point. He knows his health is somewhat precarious, but he also knows that by going to cardiac rehab, he can reverse some of the damage that has been done to his heart.

What a joy it is to see Fred had taking ownership of his behavior. Recently he initiated a conversation with his previous three wives asking forgiveness for what he had done to them and to their families. Some might say two out of three isn't bad but Fred feels a lot of pain because the first wife would not hear his confession nor accept his wish for forgiveness.

Fred has many losses that he grieves. His father, mother, brother, best friend and others that he was close to died, mostly as a result of the kind of addictive behavior he had in the past. He is very grateful to be currently finding support at church. He and his girlfriend have a solid relationship now based on their faith journey.

One time, on a trip through Ohio, the dog sitting on the front seat with him, became very agitated. Fred assumed that the dog needed to go out for a walk. He got out of the truck with Sasha and realize there was a tornado heading in his direction. He realizes now that Sasha saved his life. Over the years, Sasha spent eleven years with him in the truck. Fred relates other incidences in Oklahoma, Iowa and Kansas where the weather became very unpredictable and he experienced several close calls with serious weather.

Fred frequently refers to gratitude he has that this dog saved his life. By noticing unique behavior, the dog got the attention of his girlfriend, who saw that Fred really needed help. He is now singing **Praise God from Whom All Blessings Flow!**

24

He is in a better place

A man is standing next to the open casket where his wife of 60 years lies for viewing. People walking through the receiving line may say some of the following phrases:

"I know just how you feel."

"She is in a better place now."

"She looks so good in the casket" (cosmetology can do wonders).

When a person dies, many decisions have to be made. The same is true for our dogs. Do we bury them? Do we have them cremated? Our first dog was cremated. The next three died around age six after each of them had gone to Camp Jay whenever we were out of town, thus they had a second home there. Muffy and Zoe are buried in Jay's garden. Toby was buried in the veterinarian's back yard next to Burr Tillstrom's dog. Burr was the creator of Kukla, Fran and Ollie, a television program many years ago.

When a person says a person or a dog is in a better place, are they not referring to heaven? Do dogs go to heaven? Dogs have a very distinct personality, but do they have a soul?

If we speak of a person going to heaven, we then refer to a process that involves acceptance of their relationship with God the Father, God the Son and God the Holy Spirit. For some it is a specific day when they accepted God in the person of Jesus Christ. Some can name the day, for others it is a lifelong process that began with their baptism, as an infant, confession of faith as a teenager and an ongoing covenantal relationship in community within the church.

As a minister, I heard the confession of a dying man seeking forgiveness for all his sins and wishing to be with Jesus forever. He died one hour later. What was missing? It was an opportunity to be in relationship with God his entire life. It would be our hope that he experiences a peace that surpasses all understanding.

What should we say when we are at the funeral home for visitation?

"No one really understands what you're going through, but if you need to talk please call."

"You are in our prayers"

"Take care of yourself"

"You are fortunate to have family nearby"

"I'm not good at preparing food, but how about me coming over next Wednesday and weeding your garden?"

When one's dog dies there is no visitation or opportunity to publicly share the grief. If a good friend calls, they most often are supportive, but even that is not guaranteed. "He was just a dog."

In writing this book, I have shared the premise of revisiting loses and grieving when a dog dies. Thus, I have heard many stories. One lady said a day does not go by that she doesn't remember her dog. In fact, she now has two dogs and that she does not look forward to the day they are put to sleep.

When we remember characteristics of the dog and their personality, are we saying the dog has a soul? Certainly, each animal has a distinct personality. Some dogs like to snuggle next to you in a chair, and others maintain their distance. Dogs respond out of operant conditioning. We might speculate some breeds are smarter than others. Yet, the dog cannot comprehend the concept of heaven. Is there a place called, "dog heaven?" I could go along with that concept.

I was called upon to do a committal for a woman who had in the casket with her, the family dog cremated, and her husband cremated. Sliding the casket into the crypt, one might ask if they're all going to the same place. The man and woman have souls, and if they were in relationship with Christ, there would be some assurance of their place in heaven. The same is not true for the dog since the dog does not have language to express being in relationship with Christ. If we consider the graciousness of God, might we consider the dog also is in heaven? That is one of the mysteries for which we don't have an answer.

There are many more questions of our faith for which we don't have the answers to satisfy our curiosity. It's healthy for us to ask the questions. Asking the questions continues to help us grow spiritually.

Some years ago, our dog Toby died. My wife and I were flying to West Chester, Pennsylvania to visit our son, daughter-in-law and their two children. Our grandson called us the night before leaving and said the following: "Grandpa, when you are in the airplane, if you see Toby will you show him to Grandma?" Our grandchildren became very attached to our dogs.

They were the same breed and liked to play and to cuddle affectionately. Their grandmother was called Grandma Muffy and later, Grandma Zoe.

25

Other kinds of losses

So far in this book we have discussed the losses that come as a result of death. I'd like to explore with you, significant other area of loss. That is dealing with handicap or chronic illness.

Friends of ours had two sons with muscular dystrophy and one son with no disability. The two sons with disability have married and their wives are constant caregivers. As the boys were being raised there were many times when they were excluded from an activity because of the disability. For example, the family would go to church on Sunday, and then members of the church would be invited to other people's homes for lunch or a small snack. This family was not invited because the wheelchairs would not give entrance into their homes. This family could be the host for an activity, because their house was handicap accessible. Currently, they are looking at the overall picture of housing and realize that the condo they're living in is very much handicap accessible, but prohibits them from investing in other properties where the cost of adjusting the home to handicap accessible becomes prohibitive. When the parents were given the diagnosis of muscular dystrophy, they knew that the lifespan of these boys would be shorter than most. In no way did that stop them from obtaining advanced education. Both boys have advanced degrees, one teaching at the college level, the other teaching in the seminary after having served as a minister in a church.

This family also found that they did the majority of the entertaining because the boys could not get into the friends' homes. Often the social action occurred in a restaurant, which would be very accessible to the boys, but an additional cost factor to the parents.

Many times, boys at a young age say they would like to be a fireman. This is not realistic for these boys. The parents always attempted to show alternatives that would not crush their spirit, As the boys grew, presenting options became more difficult because of the deterioration of their health. In a number of cases, she got word that was only open for a person not in a wheelchair. One of the boys currently has only the use of one finger he can use to guide the joystick of his wheelchair. When that ability is lost he will have more difficulty with mobility. Mother explained that many times she was angry because the boys were always facing heartache.

After considerable patience, each of the boys was able to get a working dog. That meant going to training for two weeks for the family. And they had to pay for hotel rooms. It took them five years to get the first dog and three years to get the second. These dogs were called canine companions. The dog becomes a working dog for a number of years, When the dog dies, the loss is significant, because the dog not only was a working dog, but was a companion. These dogs would anticipate something their master needed. During the training these boys were able to check out a variety of dogs. Once they chose a dog, they found that the golden Labrador would best meet their needs. These boys had a grandpa who had a Yorky dog. Immediately, it adjusted to the boys being in wheelchairs and became very loyal to them. When the boys would get to the van to go somewhere, the dog was right with them, even though it was grandpa's dog. This dog tuned into the boys with unconditional love.

When a baby is born there are hopes and dreams for that child. When a child is diagnosed with down's syndrome, the reality is that there's a potential that the child would be living with them for the rest of their life. I remember reading in one of Louis Smedes books of a family in Mexico who had a down's baby. For them it meant the child will be available to work on the farm and be at home.

Where there is chronic illness, there usually is an extra amount of work for the caregiver. This takes considerable energy.

The Spoon Theory by Christine Miserandino came out in about 2003. Spoon is considered as a measure of energy. You can imagine if a person has six spoons in the morning, that as the day moves on and energy is consumed, that some people will be depleted by two in the afternoon and need to take a nap. Each day, a person will figure how many spoons they have and parcel them out as needed or required.

A young man was on a date with a girlfriend who had Asperger's syndrome. About 2 o'clock in the afternoon, she had a meltdown. The young man said to his friend "you're out of spoons, aren't you?" She said "yes" and she settled right down. The concrete nature of the spoons makes energy loss more explainable so the young lady could shift gears.

When a person is diagnosed with cancer, there is one response frequently given "I won't be able to see my grandchildren grow up." With a diagnosis of cancer, a person is frequently going to the hospital for tests, blood drawn and treatment procedures. Some of the treatment procedures last the whole day and other times a pill is taken at home. One of the losses associated with cancer is the loss of freedom to be able to make choices, with use of time and resources. Cancer treatment is costly and frequently involves transportation to a cancer center. Additionally, suggestions are made by friends and family to seek treatment elsewhere. Establishing a relationship with a doctor that is trusted is optimum for the patient and the caregivers.

Cancer presents the following potential losses:

Body changes

Need for therapy

Cost, loss of financial resources

Time

Dennis J. DeWitt

Social interaction-often a person has to be restricted to crowds or someone with a cold

There is a restriction on travel as a person needs to be close to the doctor

We used to think that cancer was only a human disease but we've learned that dogs get tumors and have cancer and we again are faced with the decision on treatments.

26

Who gets the dog?

I've heard it said that if you have a parrot, it could live for 75 years. It is then appropriate to have a life plan for that parrot, because it may outlive you.

In a recent movie, a young couple sat down to tell their dog they would no longer be living together. Who gets the dog? In this case, the couple were challenged to get counseling for themselves and the dog. One couple I know had joint custody of their cat. This was done on a weekly basis with Saturday being the exchange day. They would meet in a halfway point and hand off the cat to the person who would then have him for the next week. Would you suppose that this becomes traumatic for the cat? I think so. Cats as well as dogs get attached to the family they live with, and they notice the difference with change.

When my wife had knee surgery, our dog Zoe was beside himself, because there was a pattern of Zoe sitting next to Mary while she would quilt in the lazy boy chair. She was only in the hospital overnight, but when she returned home, Zoe was confused. Dogs many times keep score of the occupants of the home, and don't settle down until everyone is accounted for. Change can be disruptive for dogs. In addition to Mary not being there, we added in our son Jim who came home from West Chester Pennsylvania. This was a totally new person for Zoe.

One family, consists of a mother, father and two college-age boys. The dog's particular breed causes him to be a "Herder." With the family sitting on the deck, he goes from person to person, checking them out. When he is certain that everyone is there and accounted for, he will settle down and go to sleep. He will not sleep if there's a lot of activity, and the boys are only home for a short time. The dog recognizes when people are settled in and when they're on the run.

Dogs are programmed to follow certain schedules. When that changes, it takes a while to adjust. One example of that is "daylight savings time." With the time change a day starts earlier and the dog is very lethargic in the morning and can't figure out why everyone is moving so fast. When the other time change happens, the dog is up wondering where everyone else is. If the dog is used to receiving medicine at a certain time, the dog, like human beings, needs to adjust. That usually takes about a week.

I read in <u>People</u> magazine the following that illustrates the concept of custody:

> Katy Perry and Orlando Bloom are a Hollywood couple who are frequently hounded by the paparazzi, leaving the Internet wondering: are they co-parenting a pouch and are they divorcing? The stars confirmed the uncoupling and Bloom posted in Instagram with what looked like Perry's teacup poodle Nugget, After Perry appeared with a pup on Saturday Night Live in May he was photographed walking an eerily similar dog in LA. It turns out Bloom doesn't share custody of Nugget, but has been adopted a Doppelganger named Mikey. Each dog has found fame that it has appeared with Perry. Almighty has hung out with Leonardo DiCaprio and Toby McGuire.

Kathy told of her aunt and uncle in Florida who for years had conflict in their marriage. The biggest issue in their marriage was "who was going to get the dog." Finally, Jean decided that she would file for divorce and let Fred keep the dog. She decided to move to Michigan, found work there yet still maintained a friendship with Fred. Thus, when Fred had to go for an extended time on a trip, he brings the dog to Jean. The starting date for that arrangement is usually pretty clear, the end date is always unpredictable.

Kathy and her husband share a dog with her parents. That means that there are four people to share the love of the dog. It also means that when one of the couples wants to be on vacation, the other couple will take the dog.

27

Do dogs grieve?

The short answer is" yes." All we need to do is observe the action of the dog, to realize that the dog is grieving. Increased personal closeness shows that something has happened to make the dog want to be closer to us. A dog pacing back and forth shows anxiety and of course we know that the dog lacks the language to express what is going on. As stated in other places in this book, often a dog does not settle down until all the family members are present at the end of the day. Dogs can count that there are four people in the home and when one is missing the dog becomes anxious. Seeing a suitcase come out triggers, memory for the dog. The suitcase means someone is leaving.

In a condo complex in Naples, Florida there are eighteen dogs. Every day, at four o'clock, the owners of these dogs gather out in front to have the dogs relieve themselves. This is a social gathering for the adults as well as the dogs. This of course is a preparation for five o'clock cocktail hour. The dogs become attached to each other and when one is no longer there, they sense the difference. The owner of one of the dog's calls, Daisy his four-legged girlfriend. Having dinner with Daisy's owners recently, I became very aware that they mentioned the process through which they obtained the dog. This involved the evaluation process, involving an at home visit by the dog breeder. This dog flies in a chartered airplane from Michigan to Florida in the fall and spring. Does this sound like a pampered pet? Certainly. Daisy begins the evening sleeping on the bedroom floor and about four thirty in the morning she jumps on the bed to be closer to the man of the house. This man expressed how much he will miss this dog when she is gone. In 60 years of marriage, this is the only dog they have had. The woman in this case was very anxious in the beginning about having a puppy. She engaged the breeder to keep the dog for about six months so that when it was time to come to their home, Daisy was trained and showed appropriate behaviors.

These people affirmed that when they were very young, the dog staying outside was considered "property." Now their dog Daisy is very much family.

Daisy spends the day checking out the comings and goings of the family. When grandchildren come to visit, she gets very anxious if she's having to share these people with family. They see the difference in behavior when it's the "empty nest" and when visitors are present. While we were sitting on the deck and having hors d'oeuvres, Daisy was very nearby checking us out.

Some dogs in their anxiety will pace around the house. Others will either stop eating or eat too much food.

Dogs, like people are creatures of a schedule. When this schedule is changed, some adults and some dogs have greater difficulty adjusting to the change.

28

Stages of grief

Many years ago, an article on grieving written by Rev. Paul Weikert appeared in the <u>Michigan Today</u> magazine. I have gone online looking for this 1970's publication and have not found it. As a School Social Worker and later as a minister, I have used many of the steps in this document. They were helpful to people in the grief process.

These steps draw from the work of Elizabeth Kubler-Ross' <u>Ten Steps to Recovery</u>:

SHOCK AND DENIAL

When death is sudden, surrounding family members experience shock. The movements they make and the words they say sometimes don't make sense. Helping someone who has experienced loss by listening, helps them to overcome grief. According to well-trained therapists, no therapeutic counseling is helpful at this stage.

We are in a society of "denial of death." We take risks, not realizing that the consequences of our behavior might be terminal. Riding a motorcycle and weaving in and out of traffic is an invitation to serious consequences.

Many people have not made a funeral prearrangement; thus, the family is faced with decision-making while they are grieving a loss.

Jane shared with me that as she was growing up, the neighbor dog chased after her family dog. Her dog was hit by a car and died instantly. Sometime later the neighbor offered their dog to her family. She said to her parents "how could we accept a dog who caused our dog's death?

TOUCH SUPPORT

People miss being physically touched. When no one is there to kiss you in the morning or to hold your hand, you feel the loss of touch.

When my father died, my mother went to church each Sunday, knowing that one of the men of the church would put his hand on her shoulder and say, "How is it going Martha?" Many Sundays she couldn't remember the sermon substance. She would report to me that somebody cared about her. They usually did through giving expression on Sundays.

PHYSICAL SYMPTOMS

A woman whose son died of a brain tumor began to develop muscle tension in her arm. She went to a chiropractor, physical therapist, neurologist and then an orthopedic doctor. Finally, going to a psychiatrist, she and her husband were able to determine that the problem with the arm came from her inability to hold her son any longer. That physical pain was real, and several sessions with the psychiatrist helped her to understand the physiological implications of loss.

Some develop the same pain as the deceased.

ALIENATION – LONELINESS

A man driving a car says to his wife, "You want to go the highway or the scenic route?" That is a pattern for many couples, where choices are given. Sometimes traveling together can be an issue of conflict, but most often it is an opportunity for one to make a decision, often where there is some compromise. Being alone does not allow that driver to bounce something off his wife.

A person dealing with Alzheimer's finds that loneliness comes over a period of years. Sometimes a spouse says, "I just want to go to a movie with someone." This disease involves a long time saying goodbye. A husband sees his wife in the early stages, unable to make decisions, and to do the simplest tasks. Depending on how the disease progresses, personality changes occur. Often psychiatric drugs need to be administered. This means the person's personality can become very dull and they often detach even more from relationships.

In this phase, a person feels alone. Going to a restaurant is difficult because you're saying, "Table for one please."

No one to send a card to on birthday or anniversary. Doug shares with me his story.

Doug

Doug has had more than his share of grief and loss. Doug's son, David, died of a brain tumor at age sixteen. Doug and his wife Margo became very invested in a program called "Compassionate Friends." Regular meetings not only gave them the support they needed, but they were also able to reach out to others with caring. Over the years they have gained some good friends. Six months ago, Margo died of cancer. When we experience a loss, then we often revisit previous losses.

Doug is in the process of cleaning out the house, getting it ready for another son to occupy it. Doug and Margo moved into an adult housing facility with a continuing care option. Doug will now continue to live in the apartment. He is a part-time farmer. He will spend time during the warm weather, planting, attending to and harvesting crops.

Because Margo saved almost everything David owned, Doug is now sorting out not only the things that Margo had in the house, but also all of the accumulated items Margo had saved of David's. Thus, Doug continued revisiting the loss of David, and dealing with the recent loss of his wife.

One of the realities many of us experience in a situation like this is the loss of a second opinion. Often another person has a different perspective. As we interact with a spouse or children, there are times when we have to learn how to "buzz off."

A spouse may have unique fears that play out in everyday interaction. Sometimes one of the couple is most comfortable at home and shows introverted behavior, whereas the partner may find energy interacting with people. Some are very good at small talk, whereas others find situations like that draining.

As a person is working through grief, there are considerations in the rebalancing. If the deceased wife did all the budgeting and writing checks than the surviving spouse needs to sit down with a financial advisor and learn those skills. Fortunately, banks now offer bill paying services online along with direct deposit.

A component of the grief process is loneliness. There are routines that people follow each day. When that routine changes, we feel we are missing something.

At five o'clock our 95-year-old neighbor every day looked at his watch, and said it was teatime.

When it became necessary for this couple to go to assisted living, the man brought his cocktail kit along, but was told that it was off-limits. His response? "I guess my wife and I will just have to go somewhere else."

The nursing home made a variance, since they were very responsible drinkers, one having a Manhattan and the other Scotch and Water. Once they had their drink, they no longer took the car out for a ride. They were in for the night. Because this routine had gone on for twenty five years of retirement, this man was beside himself when his wife died of pancreatic cancer. He was alone, no one to drink with, no one to carry on a conversation. The man had always limited himself to one drink only but when he was alone he said he was tempted to have more than one.

Often a widow or widower is told never to drink alone. For a person alone, boundaries are hard to keep.

A surviving spouse may say that he is experiencing "loneliness." He may have a bridge group that he belongs to, or small groups, golf buddies or friendly neighbors. What he's really reacting to might be the concept of "missing." He is missing somebody to consult with. He's missing the companionship, or the fourth for bridge. Many times, it takes two people to do the driving on a trip. One person reads the map, the other one drives - a team approach.

GUILT

Some of us are really good at, "Woulda, Shoulda, Coulda;" I would have done something differently, I should have been there more, I could have looked for another doctor. All of these phrases represent unresolved issues from the past. If we say a person does their best with the given resources of energy, money and time, then we have to be able to put these feelings of remorse and guilt on a shelf.

How does one work at setting all that aside?

When I was working as an elementary counselor in the Holland Christian Schools, a fourth-grade girl talked about missing her grandfather. I asked her how she dealt with those feelings. She said: "I take the old tape out of my head and put in a fresh tape." This coping mechanism seem to be working very well for her

As noted earlier, personally, I spent two days at a silent retreat in Spring Lake Michigan. Since those days, I have felt freer, and realize that they had done the best they could with the resources they had. My mother had gone through the eighth grade and my father graduated from high school. My dad, a milkman, worked long hours starting at about 3:30 in the morning. Thus, he was in bed early at night, leaving little time for interaction. His father died when he was two years old, so he had no role model growing up. He did the best he could.

TWO KINDS OF GUILT

Realistic - When we drink and drive we are setting ourselves up for some serious consequences. "It was an accident." Being able to own our behavior allows us to benefit from therapeutic counseling. If we cannot face the music we are unable to make progress in counseling.

Unrealistic – when we take upon ourselves the responsibility of others behavior, we are putting ourselves into some unrealistic guilt.

HOSTILITY

When we become angry, we find it difficult to express that anger over losing a person. Anger, not expressed properly, can become internalized and leads to depression.

One of our parishioners said, "I'm so mad at Bob. He died first and I was left with being alone for over twenty- five years."

A 95-year-old woman in a nursing home was upset that her 85-year-old roommate "Got to go first."

JACK EXPRESSED HIS ANGER THROUGH HOWLING LIKE A WILD ANIMAL

Jack and Lisa walked a long journey together with children, dogs, and cats. Their family is very connected frequently having meals together and just spending time playing games. I have been receiving massages from Lisa for the last 25 years. Thus, I've heard stories of the family and asked if I might interview them with some of their stories. Jack has worked as an attorney for a number of years, and Lisa has worked for the Red Cross and now recently has been doing message. She's been trained as a nurse and is very close to her nursing school friends.

When asked about differences between dogs and cats they indicated cats can be by themselves during the day and evening and dogs need to be walked outdoors. Lisa appreciated the dogs, who at one time ran with her, and then in her later years, walked with her.

Sheba lived a long life. It was very painful taking her to the vet to give the dog the ending shot. Her friend Shirley said, "If Blackie or Sheba could talk would they'd say they want to continue living." Sheba couldn't make it up stairs and was incontinent. The time came to visit the vet. Jack indicated it was difficult to tell the children it was time to have it dog or cat put to sleep. Once Sheba was put to sleep they said no more pets.

I asked attorney Jack if he ever had disputes over custody of a dog. He said he had people argue over a drill or saw; he added there is sometimes significant monetary exchange over an object.

Early in our interview, I put the numbers 10 through 80 along the left-hand column and suggested that they list by the decades of their lives, losses they had experienced. Before their second decade they experienced loss of grandparents, and good friends. I then asked them to circle the most significant loss and put a box around the second most significant one.

Jack and Lisa's daughter had a problem with alcohol and for some time she was lost to the family. She went into treatment and became clean. After that she was diagnosed with cancer. The family asked me to share in their memorial service. The late Dr. Lars Granberg often said that "home is a place to be, to go away from, then come back." Their daughter was home, went away with alcoholism and came back to them clean. Then the cancer. And she died. When people in Jack's office asked him how he coped, he says he goes out to the woods and howls like a wild animal. This appears to be one way of dealing with anger because we know ***that we cannot be angry and forgiving at the same time. Our souls cannot contain both emotions together.***

PERFECTION

There are times when we have difficulty putting things into perspective, and say some of the following:

"He was the best golfer in the world …"

"She was the best cook …"

"She never got angry …"

"He was always patient with the children …"

"Her watercolors were the best in town …"

You are beginning to take stock of your loss and seeing what you miss because of the loss.

REDEMPTION

As we move along with the grief process, we come to a point where we are able to see the dead person with the good and the not so good. We accept the person as they were.

NEW LIFE

Keeping some of the past and bringing some new into your life. Some are stuck in the past and not able to move on.

RESURRECTION

Using the biblical reference as an example:

"After Jesus rose from the dead, he looked and sounded the same, but he was different — he was fuller and richer for the experience. He had scars from his wounds, but they were healed. It's the same way for us —We always have part of that loss with you, but we are alive and whole and have our own life.

In the Bible, we read the following:

John 19:17(NIV) "So they took Jesus and carrying the cross by himself he went out to what is called The Place of the Skull, which in Hebrew (Aramaic) is called Golgotha. 18 There they crucified him with two others, one on either side, with Jesus between them."

Jesus lives. Because he rose from the dead, he showed the nail prints of having been on the cross. We need to recognize those nail prints as scars on our own hands. Then, as we go through the grief process, recognize the nail print on our own hand and realize that we, through our faith, trust in God to bring healing to our losses.

Persons who are members of a faith community like the Episcopal Church, the Roman Catholic Church, Lutheran Church and many others who receive the Sacrament of the Lord's Supper every Sunday, are reminded of the suffering of Christ. In the liturgy, there is confession and absolution. There is the reminder of Christ on the night he was betrayed took the cup and the bread and said "Do this in remembrance of me."

We are reminded often of the sacrifice and yet we tend to deny that Christ came down from the cross and there would be nail prints in his hands. We don't like to talk about pain and suffering. But the image of Jesus' hands having the nail print, reminds us of our own pain and suffering. Yet there is hope.

Significant in my grief work is the hymn" Be Thou My Vision." When we sing that hymn in church, it reminds me of my wife Jan's funeral. During the singing of the hymn, I'm aware of the scar in my hand. A short time later, that scar is gone. Because her funeral was forty seven years ago, I've had some time to bring healing. The scar will always be there, but it closes over more quickly as time goes on.

This section of the book defined some stages that we go through in the grief process. We do not go through them one, two, three. We tend to go through some stages and then revisit earlier ones. Thus, there is a fluidity to the steps. The most significant of these steps is the last one where we look theologically at the death of Christ on the cross. Coming down from the cross, there are nail prints representing the scars that all of us carry. Once we reach this stage, we are then free to own our scars, and process them with a trusted person. This scar will always be there, but healing occurs.

29

What does the vet say?

Over the years we have taken our dogs to two veterinarians. Most recently, we had a good relationship with Dr. Jim Bader. When I asked him how he copes with the loss of dogs that he has seen over the years, he says he has to compartmentalize his emotions. If the dog in room one is a puppy new to a family, he shares with them in their joy. Another in room number four he has just given a shot to relax a dog and the second shot will be given to put him to sleep. This is where he has learned he must leave the emotion for number four room in that room as he enters room one, celebrating their joy.

In some cases, the owner of the dog will leave the dog at the counter and does not want to participate in the process of euthanasia. Dr. Bader's practice utilizes a technician in the room representing the family, with the doctor.

Jim was in second grade when the teacher said there were no animals in heaven. Jim's response was "If that's the case, I don't want to go there."

As he greets students, especially in elementary classrooms sharing his work as a veterinarian, Jim is often asked "what is the most difficult part of his job?" Many students would think it's euthanasia. Jim's response is "it is most frustrated when I can't figure out what is wrong with the dog to make it better."

Dogs communicate with their eyes and their tail.

Because he is very busy in his practice, Jim has learned that he refers people to outside resources for grief counseling. In West Michigan, there is a grief support group where people are invited to bring pictures and to share the hard stories about their companion animals that already died or are in the end of life stages.

Dr. Bader shared an article which occurs at the end of this book

30

Parting shots

As a minister, I work in a church where a robe is used in worship. Mine happens to be a royal blue for weekly services and a white robe for Easter, Christmas, weddings, and funerals. On Sundays, when I have been outside greeting people with a suit coat or sport coat on, I received many comments on my clothing. When the robe is worn, it becomes an equalizer. Women ministers have reported that they prefer a robe instead of having the congregation comment on their dress.

In this book, I have talked about grief issues. I would like to highlight a few thoughts in closing.

As I read in the newspaper that a person has died and there will be a memorial service at some later date, I think that stalls bringing closure. There are various reasons why people stall the memorial service; one being, it allows family to get from a distance to the location of the service. It is very helpful to have visitation and memorial service along with the reception to allow the grief process to work. Family members can support one another, and friends are available to provide support.

Considerable money is spent on funerals and some people choose not to have the money spent that way. It is very possible to have a reasonably priced funeral at somewhat lower cost.

The cost of a casket determines the total cost of the funeral. Very simple caskets function the same way as expensive ones. Visitation at the church, rather than the funeral home, becomes less costly. Ushers provided by the church save the family money. Use of a Funeral Pall covering a casket becomes an equalizer. The congregation does not focus on the cost that was put into the price of the casket. Everyone looks the same.

Cremation is an alternative to keep cost down. Some traditions do not allow this. It should be noted that unless there is a statement by the deceased, surviving family often must agree on the body being cremated.

If time is allowed for preplanning, the following information might be of help

Depending on the rules of the cemetery, a variety of tombstones can be purchased. For areas where an above ground tombstone is allowed, the family can choose something very simple or in this case a sand carved design provides decoration with the flowers and leaves. When the tombstone needs to be flat with the ground again the choice is given for style and design. Cemeteries have chosen recently to use a flat with the ground design where mowing can be accomplished without having to do a lot of trimming. In this case, a green bucket with a handle is used to place flowers on the grave site. This handle allows the trimmer the opportunity to move the flowers and mow. I personally find that plastic flowers are less than acceptable.

When the cemetery plot is purchased, built into the price is the cost of perpetual care.

How frequently do people who are grieving visit the cemetery? When there has been a recent death some go very frequently, yet this usually diminishes over time. I have been the one responsible for bringing flowers to Pilgrim Home Cemetery for my wife Jan who died in 1970. As my biological children have grown, they have taken turns bringing the flowers somewhere before Memorial Day. I would go to the Spring Lake cemetery where my parents are buried and plant flowers in a cement pot. I then would go to the Norton Cemetery to plant flowers in the larger urn, remembering my grandparents and a favorite aunt. In the process of going to Spring Lake and Norton Cemetery's I would bring along cleaning supplies to take the mold off from the tombstones.

Realizing that I was the only one going to the cemetery, I stopped bringing flowers. Occasionally I would go with cleaning supplies to take the dirt off from the tombstones.

Recently laser technology has allowed people to put a picture on the tombstone or a design such as "deer standing in the field." This one shows praying hands against a black background.

Some churches have their own burial plot for cremains. Community Church of Douglas has such a site. The names of those interred are on a bronze plaque on the wall inside the church. The cost of the bronze ribbon is $250 currently. As the cost of metal goes up, so does that cost.

Preplanning allows decisions to be made without the emotion that is normal when you are faced with making a decision in just a few days.

When considering the day of a committal, the cemetery opening and closing costs vary. If family only is present the cost is lower than having a minister speak. Saturdays usually cost more. If a burial plot is utilized for a casket, a container with cremains can often be interred in the same location. Public Cemeteries and private facilities will vary in cost.

Why is it that we still think about our last dog Zoe? She was with us for six short years. We thought she would live much longer. She was a good friend and loyal. Most of all she liked to snuggle up, sitting hip to hip in a chair. She would play ball with us. She was probably the only dog we had who would bring the ball back to us after throwing, and continue to play for longer than we would. One day she nipped at the cheek of our granddaughter. She would never do this otherwise. We recognized that she was in pain and didn't want to be bothered. Shortly after that, the vet was able to identify the pain as a bulging disc. At this point we did all financially feasible and appropriate trying chiropractic and shots all to no avail. Zoe would walk around the perimeter of our great room with her eyes saying "help me." We then made the difficult decision of having her put to sleep. We took her to the vet and she first gave her a shot to relax Zoe. She let out a heavy sigh on my lap. The vet then gave a shot to stop her heart and she was at peace. I have mentioned before that every day when the mailman comes I expect to see Zoe saying "he's here." We miss having a dog around and get your fix with grand dog Riley. It's kind of like the expression "we are glad to see the headlights but appreciate the taillights" Just like grandchildren, you can send them home.

31

Epilogue

As a volunteer counselor at the Holland Free health clinic, I learned last week about "Spoon Therapy." Spoon theory began in 2003 with a book written by Christine Miserandino. Spoon theory can best be seen as a measurement of energy expended. Each day we wake up and we have a specified number of spoons. As the day goes on, the energy is consumed and the number of spoons diminishes to a point where there are no spoons left, and it's time to take a nap. A client has a condition similar to Meniere's disease. He has frequent dizzy spells. His friend has Asperger syndrome. Both relate and support each other when they have run out of spoons.

I now wonder whether this concept would apply to grief. Some people grieve so deeply their physical manifestations of their grief being able to say in the morning I have six spoons as a measurement of energy. One can then go ahead and plan their day accordingly. Finding ways to generate energy can offset the energy draining activities. Going to a small group that is supportive can be energizing. Someone who is very needy, might suck all the energy out of you. Being able to identify the energy in something as concrete as a spoon, might be helpful. Mini vacations are helpful throughout the day. Making a brief call a phone call to a friend is one of those energizing occasions. A quiet cup of coffee with the television turned off, might be a way to escape. Too often we are glued to the cell phone or television. Someone has called that relationship a "dyad." Being consumed with texting on the dyad removes us from having to interact with others. This lack of intimacy becomes problematic for someone who is hurting for personal connections. As we grieve we find that only so many people want to listen to our story. Sometimes this sometimes requires a paid professional to move us along in the grief process. This is especially true if we feel we are ruining some of our interpersonal relationships.

How do we restore when we are depleted of spoons?

Sally's uncle died in an automobile accident. She wondered whether she should stay home or go to orchestra rehearsal where she played Viola. She chose to go to orchestra. She reflects that this got her mind off her grief, and was very energizing to her. Not only was the music restorative, but the friendships that she had in the orchestra were supportive in her grief.

Other suggestions for restoration are:

1. meditation and prayer

2. a nap

3. talking to someone you trust

The hospice organizations provide good service in this area, especially providing support groups for children and adults.

32

Veterinarian's Perspective on Saying Goodbye

By Jim Bader, DVM

Euthanasia is defined as "humanely ending a life." It is a tough decision and a major downside of pet ownership. It is the time when we are our pet's best friend, putting an end to their unnecessary suffering or pain. It is also a downside of being a veterinarian. As a veterinarian, it is my responsibility to counsel the owner as to when the time for euthanasia is near. But I am also a pet owner, so I wear both hats. The decision has never easy for my own pets and it is just as difficult to lead my clients down the path that may be best for their pet. Sometimes I have to lead myself down this path. It is never a path I relish, but it is a path that we often must take.

My job as a veterinarian has some great highs and lows. I really enjoy meeting the new puppies and the new rescue dogs with their owners. These visits with the proud owner and the new pet are some of the highlights of my day. There are smiles, questions and concerns. These are the high moments. The new owner really does not think about the day the pet will have to be euthanized; they are just looking forward to years of companionship. On the low side, there is the difficult task of euthanasia. Performing a euthanasia in one room, then switching gears to a new puppy exam in another room can be very trying. On a daily basis I have to separate the highs from the lows and go about my job. The person with the new puppy does not need to know about the difficult time in another room. I have to be upbeat and positive as I approach the happy family with their new family member. This discipline is not easy. Sometimes I must take a short break to gather my thoughts. This usually involves getting a cup of coffee our soft drink, checking my phone messages and double-checking patients in a sick animal board. This time allows me to reset my thoughts and emotions. I think checking the animals in the sick ward allows me to say to myself and my patients "I lost in exam room for but I'm doing my best not to lose with you." Sometimes the break is just a minute or two sometimes it is five minutes. I never know how long the break will be. Factors affecting the length of the age of the pet, the length of time the pet had been a patient, and how long the pet had been sick. Another factor is whether the disease is a chronic disease that was managed well, extending the pet's good quality of life. Did the pet have cancer or chronic kidney or liver disease? Was I able to manage this disease so the pet had a good quality of life? My goal as a veterinarian is to keep the pet healthy and happy. I don't want my patients in pain, feeling sick, or losing weight. I use medications and dietary management to extend the pet's quality of life. If I extended the final end point after the diagnosis from good months to hopefully a year or two, I have accomplished my goal as a veterinarian. And that makes saying goodbye to a patient a little bit easier. I often talk to students at career days and have veterinary students shadow me. I explain two facts of being a veterinarian. The first fact is the most frustrating part of doing what I do: Sometimes I know exactly what is wrong with the pet and I can't fix it. The diagnosis of severe aggressive cancer or end stage liver or kidney disease leaves me no choices but to tell the owner that there are no more treatment options available for their pet. This is just as difficult emotionally as performing euthanasia. I call the owner or go back into the exam room with the results. There is no way to "sugar coat" the news. I explain to the owner the diagnosis, offer referral to a specialist for a second opinion, and attempt to counsel the owner about the best path for their pet.

During these tense moments, I try not to have the owner make any rash decisions. Sometimes it is clear that the owner expected the horrible news; sometimes it is a surprise. If the owner is expecting bad news, I can see the expression of acceptance on their face. The owner just needed a confirmation of what they expected. The surprise diagnosis brings a look of shock to the owner. I can tell these owner's minds are racing, searching for reasons why. After talking with these owners about their options, I ask them to call me or stop in to talk in one to two days. I tell them they are only hearing every third word I say. They will go home, start to think, and then go, "What did he say about that, this or the other thing?" I speak later with these owners, trying to find the best options for their pet once the emotions have settled.

The second fact of being a veterinarian: Sometimes I am surprised. This happens often when I know the pet has a growth in the abdomen. After performing lab tests, radiographs, and ultrasound to paint a better picture of what is happening in the abdomen, surgery may still be necessary to repair the problem. As we prepare the per for surgery, I look at my staff member or student and explain a very important fact. Every time I perform a surgery like this it is like a Christmas present. You suspect what you will find, you hope to find something better, but sometimes you don't get what you want for Christmas. I always hope for the middle option, I expect the first option, and I dread the final option. But no matter what option, I hope I can repair it.

As a veterinarian, saying goodbye to a patient is never easy. It is even more difficult when it is one of my own pets. I am not only the veterinarian that makes the diagnosis, but I am the pet owner "hearing" the diagnosis. The veterinarian side is stoic and analytical; the owner side is emotional and disbelieving. Sometimes these two sides conflict, sometimes they agree, and sometimes I need my wife to bring both sides into agreement. Sometimes I frustrate my wife because I give her answers as if she is a client, trying to lead her down the path instead of just saying the quality is gone and it is time.

Some of my own pets have affected me more than others. Some of my pets have had chronic disease that I have managed well medically. I know I have helped them, and their quality of life has been good for an extended period of time. I know their final day will come. I always hope that day will be far off but if It is soon, I can accept that. When my pets have histories that are not so comfortable, these situations affect me more. I find this to be true when I think about my patients, too. When a pet comes through so much and finally "hits the jackpot" of comfort, only to face euthanasia, it pains me even more.

My wife and I just lost a very special pet that had a brief history with us but a long history before we adopted him. My wife and I volunteer at an animal shelter in Guatemala. Zunil, our new pet, was at the shelter in 2005. We estimated him to be about nine years old. He adopted my wife, following her everywhere on the shelter grounds. He would not go back to his pen unless my wife brought him back to his pen. My wife and I decided to bring him home because very few people say 'I want to adopt a pet that will only live for three to five years," He also came with a story: he was found in the area of Atitlan Panabaj a month before our visit.

This area of Guatemala was ravaged by a hurricane. Three days later, an earthquake in the area caused a landslide destroying the entire town, which has been designated as hallowed ground. The Guatemalan government started feeding the surviving dogs meat laced with strychnine to make the area "sterile." Zunil was one of the fortunate dogs removed from the area before he ate the tainted meat. He had an arduous trip from Guatemala to our home due to uncooperative airlines. When I neutered him, I also obtained some radiographs. The radiographs revealed he had been traumatized once or twice with a healed fractured femur and pelvis. Through all this he always wagged his tail, wanted petting, and never met a bit of food that was not his friend. He was the perfect pet and earned the nickname Speed Bump because you always had to step over him if he was lying down, no matter where he was. And nobody provided a better prewash for the dishwasher than Zunil. He left us suddenly due to acute liver lymphoma. He was only sick for two days. I am grateful it was sudden, but I will always miss our little Speed Bump. Zunil's early life was difficult. I am sure he survived due to his great temperament, and he lived his last three years in the lap of luxury. At least he enjoyed comfort for the last three years.

Losing a pet is never easy. There is no right or wrong answer about when to euthanize a pet. Everyone has their own idea about when and why, and these personal views should always be respected.

I once had a client explain to me something very important. He told me when he leaves his deathbed and this world, he will meet all his pets again. I like to think that all my pets — and my patients — will be waiting for me, too. I hope they greet me with kindness. I know Zunil will be there, and I expect him to be wagging his tail. His first question will be "When are you going to load the dishwasher?"

Dr. Jim Bader is a CG regular contributor.

1   LIST YOUR LOSSES BY DECADE

Begin by listing the numbers

10

20

30

40

50

60

70

80

90

Draw a circle around the most significant loss and a rectangle around the second most significant loss

In which decade did most of the losses occur?

Is there any "take aom this activity?

Name the event and any "helps" you had.

About the Author

Rev. Dennis J DeWitt was born and raised in Muskegon Heights, Michigan. His college years were split between Muskegon Community College and Hope College in Holland Michigan.

After ten years of teaching Spanish in the West Ottawa School District in Holland, he enrolled at the University of Michigan and obtained a Master's Degree in School Social Work. With this he returned to West Ottawa, for the next two decades. Many of his students were challenged with special needs. The social work job included coaching parents, helping them in setting boundaries, improving their parenting skills and dealing with loss.

In 1992, Dennis attended the first "Men's Conference" at the Crystal Cathedral, where he heard a call to ministry. He retired from the public-school system, and enrolled at Western Theological Seminary, where, in 1996, he was awarded a Master's Degree in Religious Education.

The Rev. Dr. Dan Miller of the Nondenominational Community Church of Douglas (Michigan) called him to interview as part-time Associate Pastor. Dennis began a program in the Reformed Church in America called "The Approved Alternate Route," and was ordained as a Minister in the Reformed Church in America in 2003. At the time of his ordination, he was diagnosed with Parkinson's Disease, which continues to be controlled at this point with medications.

Grief counseling services became one of his most frequently provided ministry. His personal journey began when his wife, Jan, died in 1970 of breast cancer. He was immediately thrust into the role of being a single parent with four children, ages seven, five, three and eight months. Who counsels the counselor? He sought help from friends and two clergymen. A new marriage brought three more children into the flock. This newly blended family then had seven children under age eight.

Now, years later, the family numbers 19 grandchildren and five great-grandchildren. With them have come the joys and sorrows of having many pets – dogs, to be exact. This book was generated, in part, from the experience of losing our dog, Muffy, which brought about my realization that in this process, one revisits previous losses. As with all people, the longer one lives, the more those losses accumulate.

The stories contained in this book are for the most part real and true and represent many interviews.

Rev. Dennis J. DeWitt. October 2016. A prayer for peace for a family at the end of a memorial service. Note that the stole contains many symbols. This was made by my wife's quilt group over 20 years ago. A minister's stole is a symbol of servanthood.

Jim, our technology guru at Community Church of Douglas said the following:

> *Pastor Dennis must really like dogs since he has to change the master password every time he gets a new dog. I can recall at least three of his dogs we used- Toby, Muffy and Zoe.*

MAY THE LORD BLESS YOU AND KEEP YOU. MAY THE LORD SHINE HIS FACE UPON YOU AND GIVE YOU PEACE FROM NOW AND EVERMORE. AMEN

Printed in the United States
By Bookmasters